Understanding the French

Elliot Paul

Under-standing the French

Random House   New York

Contents

Understanding the French

1. *Liberty, Equality and Fraternity*

The French are individualists. As a nation they are held together by natural frontiers on two sides, and exposed along more than half of their border lines to hostile attack by tribes that are decadent on the south, savage to the east, and undependable to the north. The population is slightly under 43,000,000, the continental area 212,659 square miles, about 200 persons to the square mile. The density of population in France is, roughly, about one-fourth that of England.

Germany has 67,000,000 Germans, crowded into living room just over one-half the area of France.

Liberty, equality and fraternity has been the slogan of the French since the Revolution. To the east, long before Hitler, no such triad of principles was allowed to interfere with the will to power.

To the south, authoritarianism, and to the north, across the channel, political intrigue and the jugglery of the balance of power have kept France between the devil and the deep blue sea. Yet France does not consider herself circumscribed. She reaches out to her colonies, which include Algeria, French Equatorial Africa, French Guiana, French India, French Oceania, French Somaliland, French Sudan, French West Africa, French West Indies and French Indo-China. There is also the French administrative zone in the Sultanate of Morocco and the protectorate of Tunisia.

The total population of France, its possessions out of Europe, its colonies, administrative areas and protectorates reaches 111,000,000, in an area of 5,000,000 square miles. The British Commonwealth has 619,178,882 people in 12,993,272 square miles. The United States and possessions have a population of 158,000,000 in 3,600,000 square miles.

The principal ancestors of the modern French, the Gauls, were distinguished among the tribes of Northern Europe in the pre-Christian era, and for some time after Christ, by a tendency to carry their enthusiasms to extremes. Perhaps it is better to say that the Gauls were capable of enthusiasms which did not plunge them into the depths of fanaticism. They were brave to the point of rashness, and suffered because they did not always allow for possible consequences—a trait for which they were as lovable then as they are today.

Gauls not only loved independence, but they fought to have and hold it. When the choice lay between liberty and death, a few won liberty and many drew death. Those who survived carried on the ideal. That, in brief, is the history of freedom.

The same process is repeated today in Spain, where small bands of Asturians in the mountains, of undercover patriots in Madrid, of fugitives in the woods of the Balearic Islands, continue the fight against the tyranny of Franco, imposed by Hitler and Mussolini. They are forsaken and slandered by fellow democrats and high churchmen. But they are fed and protected by true Spaniards who are waiting, who have long been waiting, and, alas, have long to wait.

To the hot Celtic blood of the Gauls were added the tempered and civilized strains of the Romans and the Franks. From the Romans, as pointed out so aptly by Philippe Lefrançois, a contemporary French essayist with exceptional sensitivity and balance, the Gauls and associated tribesmen learned the love of order, which was not carried to excess; a fondness for clearly defined law, which has made the French language the tongue of diplomacy; and the unifying impulse of an abstract conception— The State. That any people, generally speaking, are inclined toward consideration of the abstract, puts them on a very high plane. The modern French are brave, they must have freedom, and they are outstandingly intelligent. I failed to mention in my earlier paragraph about the Gauls that they were naturally polygamous. No people have more effectively resisted the pressures of Church, State, mechanics or superstitions than the French, who have thereby escaped the more degrading features of monogamy. They have that solid institution known as "the family," yet the male members, at least, are not brutally restricted. The French nation, by and large, is not degenerating into a nest of neurotics and psychopaths because of sex repression. In that respect, they are chips from the old Gallic block.

The Franks, from whom is derived the name "Francia" or France, "exerted a humanizing influence with their concrete conception of a social hierarchy based on the feudal bond between man and man, between overlord and vassal." When central authority loses its grip, as it does periodically in the history of any people, the interdependence of man on man in a community, as practiced and transmitted by the Franks, enabled the provinces and regions of France to organize defenses which saved the best of them from extinction at the hands of the worst.

I was in Paris in 1937, at the time of the great international exposition on the Champ de Mars.

War was approaching; the national economy was volcanic and strained. International chicanery never before or since reached such heights and depths. Hitler was ranting about living space, which turned out to be dying space for friends and enemies alike. Mussolini was boasting that he had "put an end to what had been known as 'civilian' life," i.e. from the point of view of free self-respecting men the only kind of life worth-while to ancient Gauls or present-day Frenchmen, British or North Americans. Still Paris threw off her depression, conquered her misgivings, and had a jolly good time. The French, knowing every German with a camera or notebook was a Nazi spy, admitted them in droves and let them do their worst. The French have such a deep-rooted contempt for German efficiency that they assume it will always, over a period of time, react against itself and, like Pope's wounded serpent, will bite itself and inject its own venom into the Prussian state.

Having been the victims of Hun aggression as far back as their national memory goes, the French aversion to Germans and all things German is basic in an otherwise generous national character which takes to its bosom all the rest of mankind. The French permit themselves this one exception. They love humanity, but question the admissibility of the German to that brotherhood. The average Frenchman or Frenchwoman cannot be made to believe that Germany, however supervised or partitioned, will really disarm, or that any German army, permitted to be organized under whatever high-sounding defense purpose that can be formulated by naïve Anglo-Saxon statesmen, will take orders from anyone except those high in their own military hierarchy.

How differently the French feel about their colonials, and the inhabitants of their dependencies and protectorates! The skin of Northern Frenchwomen is clear, cool and pale; that of Southern Frenchwomen is tinted on the brunette side and, at the drop of almost any article of clothing is suffused with life and warmth. The Frenchman of the streets and fields finds any unusual color of skin fascinating. The exotic is stimulating and interesting. At the sight of a woman of another race or climate, a Frenchman has the liveliest desire to embrace or possess her. Now this holds true in many other lands but less in England than elsewhere. However, most white women, the world over, feel a strong hesitancy in actual contact with darker men of other races. The world tendency certainly is for the red, black and yellow races to approach nearer the white, in pigmentation, through natural instinctive selection in breeding. Frenchwomen, and I do not mean only those of easy virtue, but the workers, housewives and society matrons, are more curious than women of other countries about ac-

tual intimacy with exotically colored men. They
suspect that if their men find miscegenation delightful, the thrill may carry both ways. Who is bold
enough to reject such a thought? The risk of
breeding children doomed to hurt and bewilder-
ment has a deterrent effect, but nowhere outside
France has the practice of contraception been practiced more carefully, skillfully or effectively than
among the women of France, high and low, rich or
poor, although of course in France, as elsewhere,
the high and rich have a considerable advantage.

The French are realists, a practical people. They
learned, centuries before Dostoievsky, that one
must select from his or her desires before gratifying
them. Some adventures are all right to think about,
as long as one thinks clearly. While the Colonial
Exposition was the rage of Paris and of France,
unprecedented numbers of natives from Guinea,
Guiana and Inini, from Chad, Gabon, Ubangi-Shari
and the Congo, from Chandernagore, Karikal,
Mahé, Pondicherry and Yanaon, from Morocco,
the Marquesan Islands, Somaliland, Senegal and
Mauritania, Dohomey, Niger and Dakar, from
Guadeloupe and Martinique, Tunisia and Algeria,
Cochin-China, Annam, Cambodia, Tongkin, Laos
and Kwangchowan, were camped on the southeast
outskirts of Paris and roamed the Paris streets by
night and day, in costumes transceding the imagination of French *couturiers*, who lead the civilized

world. None of the female natives lacked tempta-
tions of the most eloquent and extravagant kinds.
The black, tan and gold-skinned men fared not
nearly as well, but still came in for much flattering
attention and scattered opportunities to extend the
horizon of their social experience. Few of either
sex departed exactly as they had arrived.

The French are the world's greatest at staging
World's Fairs and Expositions. I feel a thrill of
pride to this day, fifty-four years later, when I remember that a painting I did at a Massachusetts
public school was exhibited at the great Paris Exposition of 1900. The French do not have billions
at their disposal, when they go on one of these
world cultural sprees, as do the promoters in the
United States. But they have taste, inspiration, and
that fine old heritage of group enthusiasm inherited
from the Gauls. The sense of double-entry bookkeeping which has come down to them from the
Franks somehow got lost in conflict with the Roman extravagance taught by the cohorts of the
Caesars. I doubt if anyone knows how much or
how little the Colonial Exposition of 1931 cost,
and, what is more important, nobody cares.

The French have a most elaborate fire department, which is a branch of the Army. Because Paris
firemen, or *pompiers*, rate free admission when assigned to theatres, concerts, lectures and the like,
and the duties before the liberation were practically

nonexistent, the elders of wealthy families used to try, when their sons were drafted for their compulsory military service, to get them assigned to the Paris Fire Department. Since the war, some antisocial Army worthy, who probably never saw service with the Resistance or on any active front, set up an elaborate schedule for the physical culture of young firemen, so that the *pompiers*, when last I saw them, were spending more than half their time performing setting-up exercises and running through the quarter in shorts and sneakers. It is difficult to decide which they hated most—the physical exertion, the exposure to ridicule or the author of the plan.

While the famous Colonial Exposition was in full blast, another enterprising branch of the government propaganda service induced the Fire Chief to invite the heads of fire departments in other principal cities throughout the world to send delegations of firemen and examples of their latest equipment to Paris for a grand convention and competition. Now up to that time I had lived in Paris for fifteen years and I could remember having witnessed only one dangerous or destructive fire. The new Salle Pleyel burned while it was in process of construction. Two persons lost their lives, and one of those was an American. Parisians do not create fire hazards because they waste no inflammables or rags. Most of the medieval buildings are of stone or plaster, not wood, and someone always seems to be on hand with a pail of water when a little flame gets started. However, while the cream of the Fire Department of Paris was on the Cours la Reine, vying with firemen from Berlin, Prague, New York, London and Rotterdam (among others) in playing streams of water across the river Seine, the Dutch exhibit at Vincennes, including wonderful full-size replicas of East Indian architectural marvels, was burned to the ground. The loss was inestimable!

That is the way with exhibitions, when organized by the French. The accidental features often surpass those announced.

In the few minor instances when French firemen are turned loose on a building in which a fire, however tiny, seems to have started, the destruction and havoc they raise is a lesson to the negligent for generations to come. One can readily understand that when a fireman, dressed to kill with brass helmet and vermilion pants, has his chance to wield an axe, extend a ladder, or play a hose in earnest, he is not going to do it lightly. He is going more or less berserk. If the blaze is high in a building, all the apartments or stores below are drenched and ruined, and the law courts are jammed for years, deciding who, if anyone, pays. In World War I, some general got the bright idea of sending Paris firemen to various fronts for flame-throwing and incendiary service. One and all, the *pompiers* showed more aptitude in setting conflagrations than they had in extinguishing inconsequential fires at home.

Now consider the French population, descended from Gauls, Franks and renegade Romans who became victims after being victors, in contrast with the United States' melting pot of white malcontents and restless types, with an underprivileged resentful black population of 11 per cent, and one citizen in seventeen slated for a psychiatrist's couch. The middle-class French would all hang from chandeliers and chatter in a body rather than pay for psychoanalysis, which they get from the more sensitive priests free of charge. The French worker has to be able to think fairly straight to keep alive; the wage scales are so low and he is so little esteemed. The French aristocrats admit they are decadent, anachronistic and parasitic, and they like being that way. But wherever you find a Frenchman you will find a man who accepts folks of other nations and races (barring the Germans) and never has to condescend. The blackest of statesmen from Central Africa or Martinique are trained for government service and in Paris are admitted, like any men, to hotels, restaurants and salons. The sight of Josephine Baker taking tea at the Ritz with the Duchess of Rohan would excite no flurry or comment.

Concerning white North Americans, the French

are baffled. The reports they get from French travelers in the United States are more or less jumbled together in their minds, with little regard for chronology. Thus a trivial observation by Paul Claudel is likely to be confused with the early writings of a Jesuit missionary of the seventeenth century. Not thirty years ago, French newspapers ran pictures of Caillaux and his colleagues on the war-debt mission eating grapefruit in Washington. The outsized citrus fruit exemplified the drolleries of a rich people who voluntarily swallowed acid for breakfast, instead of munching crisp golden-brown *croissants* with *café au lait*. When lynchings are reported from the South, the French accept them as they would reports of frontier troubles incident to the Gold Rush. If an *echt* Britisher boasts of having thrashed a punkah wallah on the steps of his club in Rumblebellipore, the French suspect that Pakistan is inadequately policed due to lack of American funds. Up to the outbreak of World War II, it cost twenty-five francs as a fine if one man struck another in public. That is why Anglo-Saxons were so puzzled when they saw French taxi drivers and their clients, for instance, shouting the strongest invectives at each other for fifteen minutes at a stretch, without violence or bloodshed. Each shouter was waiting for the other to hit him first, and make himself subject to the fine of twenty-five francs.

I am not sure that the law covering the above contingencies has ever been repealed or amended. Twenty-five francs today would amount to about seven cents.

2. *French Food*

While Paris contains a large share of the finest restaurants in the world, the cuisine offered in any one of those establishments is likely to be regional. The restaurant, as an institution, is of comparatively recent origin in France, dating back only to the period just after the first revolution when the Bastille was torn down. Formerly the fine cookery which has placed France far ahead of any other nation in the field of gastronomy took place in castles and chateaux. When aristocrats had to flee or go into hiding, the domestics who had cooked for them either founded eating houses or got jobs in those of more enterprising displaced servants.

Too much stress has been laid by writers, by and large, on the fancy eating that tourists and rich

Frenchmen do in Paris, and the famous restaurants of Dijon, Lyons, Toulouse, Marseilles and Rouen. The significance of food in France is the fact that the French, generally, are well nourished and at a surprisingly low cost.

In the regions devoted to agriculture—that is to say, nearly all of the country—the peasants enjoy a varied, balanced diet, well flavored with aromatics, pungents, condiments, spices and wine. Farm women have passed on their skill and knowledge through generations that span twenty centuries and nearly every kind of governmental evolution or experiment. The inexpensive cuts of meat, the innards, faces, brains, ears, glands and tails, have been composed into traditional dishes—stews, soups, scallops, rice dishes, sausages, creams and grills. The best of the French sauces are enjoyed in peasant houses. Voltaire rated the English as a droll people who had fifty-seven varieties of religion and only one sauce, presumably Worcestershire.

The French farmer, stock raiser, forester or market gardener has a simple breakfast of home-baked bread or rolls with coffee. Mid-morning indigestible hot biscuits are practically unknown in rural France. Our French "son of the soil" takes a few minutes off to drink a glass of wine and eat another piece of bread. The noon meal will feature beef in wine, in the Burgundy or Bordeaux style, braised ox joints, lamb shanks, a kidney stew, a *matelote* of fish or eels, or some other hearty dish involving a sauce to be soaked up with potatoes or bread. Often a vegetable will be served as a separate course, string beans or green peas, for instance, or flageolets, oyster plant, eggplant, spinach, *oseille aseille*, dandelion or other greens, *sauté*. The crudest peasant, farthest removed from Parisian high culture, does not relish, any more than does the President of France, having his vegetables splashed on the same plate with a carefully flavored sauce unrelated to them. Your Frenchman likes to taste each item at its best, and not in haphazard or incongruous combination.

Between the vegetable and the cheese a green salad will be served as a refresher, and the dressing will be of olive oil and wine vinegar, about three to one in that order, enhanced by salt and freshly ground pepper. With the cheese goes another draught of wine. A peasant will drink between a half-liter and a liter with each of his two main meals.

Comes the eventide, and your Frenchman of the country will have soup, cheese and, possibly, a sweet or savory dessert. The soup will not be poured from can to pan to soup tureen. It will contain, along with the tangible ingredients, much love and delicacy, much vigor and arrangement. The principal French soups are black bean or lentil soup, soups of the cabbage family which are never held over a day, a thick St. Germain, clear bouillons and consommés, so disarming in appearance, so profound in richness and flavor. The cream soups of shellfish, vegetables and poultry, the turtle soups, onion soups, oxtail soups, pepper pots, mutton broths, marmites, macaroni and noodle soups, all are designed as complete, satisfying digestible meals not calculated to disturb a night's sleep soon to follow.

France has appreciated and created good nourishment so long that one has the feeling, in the country or the slums of the city, that ideal gastronomy has transcended, somehow, its living human agents. It is as if France, herself, that dear abstract mother of us all, is thinking and planning the meals, which occur as clouds beautify the dawn or the twilight. It seems, at mealtimes, as if man and nature had agreed to a truce, the one to pay attentive tribute, the other to provide without guile.

I think the greatest disaster ever to inflict itself on my own beloved country, the United States, was of a negative nature. George Washington was forming his first cabinet. In Philadelphia, exiled and ready for employment was the French gastronomer, Brillat-Savarin. Had the Father of our Country made use of Brillat-Savarin, had Brillat-Savarin been our first secretary of provender and nourishment, had our America, making its historical start and noblest experiment, been organized by that genius, so that proper attention would have been given our food production, distribution, preparation and consumption, at the same time that our new politics were sprouting—what could we not have done?

Instead, improvisation, disorganization, confusion and continuous colossal waste. The difference between alimentation in France and in the United States is like the difference between a basket of eggs spilled on concrete and an *omelette aux fines herbes.*

I have described ordinary country eating in France. In Paris and the other cities, the white-collar class and the small proprietors do as well as the peasants, and enjoy even more variety, so well are the city markets organized. The Anglo-Saxons muddle along with ulcers, indigestion and colic, never learning or progressing; in fact, going steadily from bad to worse as the machine age continues and the atomic age, by man's stupidity and meanness, is retarded. If atomic power gives mankind leisure, at long last, men cannot employ it better than in the improvement of food. The best traditions have come to us from the Sumerians, the Egyptians, the Greeks and the Romans in turn, and now rest with the French. They are ours for the asking. Their quality is neither limited nor strained.

It would be too bad to leave the subject of food in France without a word about Belley, a town in

the department of the Ain, within sight and shelter
of the snow-topped French Alps and near the great
marshes of the Rhone, south of the Burgundy wine
region. Belley is familiar to world readers who
never have been there because it is the county seat
described so aptly and in such artistic detail by
Stendhal in *The Red and the Black*. The characters
in that great novel were taken from life, in Belley.
Today the town is well supported by a couple of
thriving silk factories. White oxen tread the hills,
yoked in pairs. Each Monday is market day and
farmers bring their wares and livestock to the market town, branding their pigs with a homemade
vegetable dye like Tyrian purple.

There still is an important military post there,
with a garrison from which each member would
deplore a transfer or discharge.

It was four miles from Belley where Gertrude
Stein had her country residence, a house she wanted
so badly before she could buy it that she went to
the Secretary of War himself, in order to pave the
way for the deal. The house was occupied by a
major who had been overlooked two or three times,
for one reason or another, when promotions were
in order. The Major would not sell his house for
any price unless he was made a lieutenant-colonel
and transferred to Northern Africa. Now Gertrude, with Alice Toklas, had performed such he-
roic ambulance-driving duty in World War I that

she had been cited and decorated by the same Secretary of War, who was still in office when she coveted the Major's little house. Gertrude, always a woman of direct action in the higher echelons, went straight to the Secretary and asked him to arrange the Major's promotion, which he did.

Before Gertrude and Alice got the house, they spent their summer holidays at the Hotel Pernollet, in Belley. She liked the place so well she recommended it to me and my stay with Pernollet VI as host was memorable. The cooking and service of the owner-chef was renowned throughout Europe and for several generations European gourmets had been making pilgrimages to Belley, the birthplace of Brillat-Savarin, who was for many years the town mayor. The Hotel Pernollet's semi-wild asparagus tips in the chef's special sauce were of such quality that ordinary asparagus in standard sauce was not palatable for months after. For dinner my first evening there I had goose, stuffed with wild hare, which in turn was stuffed with a squab.

It was traditional with the Pernollets that when the elder reached the age of sixty, he would retire to a nearby private apartment connected with the hotel but having a separate kitchen. That summer Pernollet VI cooked for the hotel and his father, Pernollet V, cooked for himself. At lunch time and dinner time the best of the townsmen would promenade past the two kitchens, inhaling and sampling the aromas from each in turn. They would argue about the respective merits of Pernollet V and Pernollet VI as chefs. In extreme cases, when the odors were especially rare and freighted, partisans of the father and the son would come to blows.

And in the public square across the way, between the hotel and river, with the Alps—the pass called *Col du Chat*—for a backdrop, was a statue of Brillat-Savarin. I could not help making my obeisances at the shrine which commemorates the patron saint of all gourmets.

Reader, I wish you well. I wish that you may be in Belley and that wonderful region some year in the late autumn, when the stock raisers and wine growers band together, with their women and children, to burn the dry, sweet grass which cloaks the great marshes. The men, Allobroges, tend the fires, which for me have a scent beyond the perfumes of Arabia, and they feast on wild game and domestic beasts and fowls. They drink hogsheads of new wine—the Côtes de Nuits, the Côtes de Beaune, Pommard, Chambertin, Mâcon, Beaujolais. Hosanna! The glow of the embers at twilight is reconciled with the tinted clouds of sunset, and the smell of roast meats, pungents and charred grass and the gleam of the Rhone and the sky and the Alps, around the French, leave an impression of cosmic unity and universal harmony which, because of its theoretical structure beneath the transient light and sound waves, endures, world without end. There can be no world without France. Amen.

5/5/57 Mess

N 8.010

T.

Checked Out

The policy of the French is love and let love. They are not angered or offended if individual men love women, men, girls, boys, horses, elephants or butterflies, in any known style. However, when any foreigner, man or woman, professional or amateur, practitioner or *animateur*, shows piquant imagination with regard to the perpetual skirmish, your true Frenchman, from oaf to savant, in garret or official bureau, perks up and demonstrates a lively interest in the affair, even if said interest must, perforce, be academic.

The French approve of love. They recognize it as a force which is here to stay, in spite of the prodigious volumes of nonsense theologians have heaped around *l'amour* in an effort to classify it with low-grade sins. In the laws of France are provisions for special consideration of crimes of passion, that is, of deeds of violence committed under the black spell of jealousy, of love frustration, of the pain and fire which make demons of men, furies of women and victims of resultant children. Knowing full well that a spark of love, igniting one heart from another, may land the partners, each and severally, on a slab in the morgue, in jails and dungeons, in hospitals or asylums, in monastic seclusion or immersion in alien crowds, Frenchmen and women accept *l'amour* as the one phenomenon or heavenly caprice which makes life and existence on this planet an adventurous, endurable affair.

I have stood in museums throughout France and watched the unmated women, the displaced females, the housewives—the backbone of France when eyes are ceilingwards—the bourgeois men, the "Sunday Frenchmen" who are idle and find room with relatives on weekdays but on Sundays, when other men are at home, are in the way. Whenever any of the aforementioned, or any of their compatriots unclassified, noticed a large painting on Original Sin, with Adam, Eve, Jahwe and the snake, the French beholder indulged in a tolerant passing smile, as if the artist had had his tongue in his cheek. The muddled theological pronouncements on sex, or love, the stigma the clergy has tried to attach to the act which gives us our only chance for birth, have made it impossible for

the descendants of the polygamous Gauls, the
neighbor-loving Franks and the empire-building
Romans to become saturated with religion to the
exclusion of independent sense. The French take
what the Church has to offer, make use of what
fits their situation, pass lightly over the rest that
does not seem to make sense, and if the organized
clergy gets too powerful and obstreperous, find
some legal way to slap them down. Church buildings, the great cathedrals as well as the rural mon-
strosities almost as grotesque as the Italian "Houses
of God," are the property of the Government of
France and are leased to the Church during good
behavior. The French, including the most outspok-
enly and actively anticlerical among them, have no
objection if Catholic couples or mixed Catholic-
agnostic couples go through any number of religious ceremonies, providing such rites do not
involve sights, sounds or odors which might constitute a public nuisance. However, the only legal
marriage in France is the civil ceremony, at which
the mayor of some *commune* or *arrondissement*
presides.

The public-school system of France is in no way
dominated by the Church. In villages, most of the
schoolteachers are freethinkers and conduct running discussions, in the presence of parents and pu-
pils, with village priests, throughout their terms of
office. There is little or no attempt on the part of

French school authorities to set kids right or wrong about *l'amour*. The teachers know all too well that little Jean or Yvonne, aged nine, may know more about the principles and practices of love than the school superintendent does.

There are few writers in any country more worthy of attention and admiration than André Gide or Henri de Montherlant. When Gide depicts a mature homosexual male terrorized and black-mailed by small French boys of good family, all of us who know Paris or Concarneau or Belley or Avignon realize that the author is on firm ground. Boys will be boys, and if they learn that by threat-ening to denounce an innocent pansy, charging that he has accosted them, they can reap a rich harvest, they may take advantage of the opportunity until they are old enough to understand what cruelty means. De Montherlant has some of the dear kiddies stealing letters ready for the mail in order to steam off the stamps and resell them for pin money. The kids read the letters in question before they destroy them, and if they find clues for blackmail opera-tions, some adults are in a bad spot.

Still, those ultra-sophisticated French youngsters pay no attention to ordinary love affairs, providing the principals have no reason for keeping the liaison secret. And in the higher grades and the *lycées*, necking is only a means to an end. Frank Harris and others have written about minor atrocities committed by the stronger boys on the weaker in English schools. Similar conditions obtain in French schools, especially in the theological seminaries, where vice seems the more delicious if only because its sinful aspects are stressed.

When Shakespeare wrote that "All the world loves a lover" he must have been thinking about France. In America and to a degree in England, a lover is an object of suspicion and mild revulsion if he is demonstrative in public. The French understand that love is contagious. Rabelais wrote about a magic cloak Panurge smuggled into the village where the Passion Play was being performed, so that apostles, Romans, scribes, Pharisees and thieves, as well as all animals and insects within range of the spell abandoned whatever they had been doing and started making love. Young children as well as old folks in France grasp the symbolism and are glad that man is frail and woman supposedly is frailer.

Never have I been more humiliated than I was one night on the Perpignan to Paris express (from Barcelona). I had the lower berth of a sleeping compartment, and when an attractive woman was presented by the harassed conductor, the latter hoping I would offer to share my quarters, the woman was slightly shocked, and demurred.

The conductor, giving me the once over, said, to reassure her, "Don't be afraid, madame. He's just an Englishman."

I spent part of the night trying to explain to my chance companion how Americans were different, but I am not sure to this day to what extent I got my point across. The lady, it turned out, was a Turk.

4. *A Note on the French and Their Dumb Friends*

Nowhere in the world are pets treated with greater respect and consideration than in Paris or the French provinces of the north. One of the few instances of extreme cruelty, in which I saw an enraged teamster maim a recalcitrant stallion with a pair of ice tongs, resulted in immediate protest and forceful intervention on the part of all bystanders within range. The impulsive teamster sustained a fractured jaw, lost part of one ear, and had his ribs kicked out of place.

Your author, in fact, set down his brief case, and was skirting the melee, albeit somewhat prudently, in the hope of getting a crack at the loathsome teamster, when it struck him that the spectacle of one of our human brethren undergoing an ordeal far stiffer than he had dealt the horse did not noticeably stir emotions of pity and compassion in the crowd. I stopped to reflect. Somebody who cared more for possessions than for either man or beast filched the brief case while my mind was groping among higher speculations.

In Southern France, even as in Italy, small donkeys are clubbed unmercifully as a matter of course, and no one seems to mind. Once in St. Tropez I saw a stray priest halt one of those sadistic outbursts by telling the peasant that his donkey, no doubt, had been doing the best he could. The peasant asked what difference it made whether a donkey, being a non-Christian, was easy or in pain.

The priest, rather slow on the uptake, could think of no effective answer to that, and wandered off, presumably to ponder the metaphysical aspects of sin and punishment in an *âne* without an *âme*.

5. *An Exquisite Superfluity*

The civilized French are in a small minority, as are the civilized in other countries. The middle class, with its worship of the mediocre, is dominant in politics and cares nothing for art. Prosperous Parisians who wish to accentuate their affluence will boast that they, or their fathers, came to the capital in *sabots*, or wooden shoes.

Frenchwomen of the lower classes who are attractive and ambitious like to be pampered by their wealthy protectors. A substantial percentage of them, having felt the horror of privation, do not accept the conventional ideal of a modest home, with a routine male provider and thankless years of living on the edge of poverty and deprivation. Soon they discover, most of them precociously, that their bodies will bring them ease and luxury far beyond anything their virtues or their intellects may command. They do not want to marry. They want to be kept—in style. They do not want to be modest and inconspicuous. They must be noticed and envied.

France thus far has no Dr. Kinsey to catalogue the habits of the French male. The country has never had an effective inquiry, but in place of figures and statistics, the literature of France has revealed most frankly the roués and courtesans. In Anglo-Saxon lands those men and women who wish to get from life an abundance out of all proportion to their contribution, with rigid class distinctions on the one hand, and melting pots on the other, are denounced by moralists, deplored by economists, and in English literature are caricatured into horrible examples, intended to convince the young that pleasure does not pay. In France the attitude is different. No French author would take delight in rendering a frivolous carefree beauty into a hideous derelict who dies in agony just to emphasize the dubious maxim that the wages of sin are death.

The symbol of man's extravagance and woman's depravity in France, where wild life maintains itself at a minimum, is the fur piece or garment. The craze for mink coats or silver-fox mantles has spread from the boulevards of Paris to the rest of the world. The precedent is found again in the Garden of Eden legend which seems to fascinate the

French from every angle. Jehovah, according to the French expert on high jinks, Alexandre Arnoux, was the first furrier. Adam and Eve, in Holy Writ, when overcome with consciousness of their nudity, fashioned garments of leaves. It was the Lord of Hosts Who found vegetable foliage inadequate as covering for His impulsive protégés, and Himself made them suits of fur, with the skin side inside. Adam and Eve accepted them and wore them. Just then they were aiming to please.

The barbarian hordes who swept over Europe wore furs because the pelts of animals afforded them the most practicable kind of clothing at negligible cost. The civilized French take particular joy in adapting anything primitive to their luxuries. Not content with pelts of lynxes, skunks, otters, minks, beavers and foxes, French furriers introduced the chinchilla, various kinds of monkeys and Chinese white rabbit in a dozen clever disguises.

About one hundred years ago no lady of easy virtue or female entertainer was complete without her massive chinchilla coat which wrapped her quite shapelessly from shoulders to shoe tops, with jacket as long as the modern "zoot suit," a fur skirt that hung like a tent, and a chinchilla cap or hat to match. One of the portrait photographs of the "Divine" Sarah Bernhardt gives her the amplitude of a large wine barrel, since Sarah's generous *embonpoint* and natural padding was widened with priceless chinchilla. Today, the styles are neater, more sightly, and in closer conformity with the human structure, like the court cloak of white ermine and black velvet made by Revillon for the former Queen Elizabeth, now Queen Mother.

Whatever the fashions, bulky and grotesque, trim and lovely, they originate with the French. The furs are smuggled from Russia, or Canada, or from almost anywhere outside the continental limits of the Republic, and quite a few enter the country legally and are sold openly. But the Frenchman who wishes to glorify his mistress and place her on the sinful pedestal she craves, if he cannot afford Revillon, Weil, or the grand furriers of the rue St. Honoré, knows his way around the Place de la République, where on upper storeys of back streets he can get for the equivalent of $100 furs that would cost $500 in the shoppers' danger zone.

The French understand all sorts of nuances in amorous relationships, and the man who pays through the nose for furs for his women is aware that the texture, the suppleness, the sheen, the softness, the durability, and, above all, that elusive, ineradicable, exciting, mildly maddening animal odor, will affect a mistress to the core of her being and pay sensuous dividends throughout the duration

Для her 2,000th "birth-day," recently passed, France's government appointed an impressive committee to compile a book. The committee consisted of celebrities, artists, writers and promoters active in the international exchange of artistic ideas, and members of honorary societies of arts, artistic trades and letters. The conservative members did not hesitate to include Paul Eluard, poet and active Communist. Under the heading "The Pleasures of Paris" the French publicists commenced with negative recommendations, to the effect that Rome is richer in historical relics, the plan of New York is more modern, the natural surroundings of Rio are more grandiose, and that *even* London has a certain charm for those who appreciate the melancholies of fog and mist.

Jean Fayard placed first in his list of attractions unique in Paris the *répétitions générales,* or dress rehearsals of theatrical productions for the benefit of critics and privileged men and women "of the world." The most amusing French motion picture I ever saw was entitled *L'Habit Vert.* In it the steering committee of the staid French Academy decides there are enough artists, poets, musicians, statesmen, pedagogues and scientists in the ranks of the "Immortals" and agree to invite a certain Count Latour-Latour, as a typical "man of the world."

By a "man of the world" the French mean one whom everyone expects to see at important social or public functions. He is a specialist in behavior, not necessarily talented artistically or profound intellectually. Of his remarks, every third or fourth must be witty. He must not be ordinary, and neither is he permitted gross eccentricities. He must be dangerous to females, without having had any scandal associated with his name. He may be rich, but seldom self-made.

The dress rehearsals for critics were discontinued in France because the theatre directors got fed up with the critics, but shows could not thrive without the old-time publicity, however unfavorable. Now certain privileged critics, who can be counted on to behave, are invited to first nights, and the rest of the house is organized by the playwright, promoter, backer or management as carefully as a for-

mal dinner party. Monsieur Fayard suggested that
outsiders, if they have the price, may wangle invi-
tations or tickets to these packed first performances
and will find a high type of pleasure in watching
the wheels go round. The critics will identify themselves by making notes with fountain pens, for the
article shortly to appear. The women will wear
evening gowns, or elegant cocktail dresses. The
"men of the world" will be in tails. The day is not
yet when bona-fide French *hommes du monde*
compromise on tuxedos with colored bow ties.
Whenever the illiterate get stuck for lofty conver-
sations, Fayard suggests that they make some re-
mark about Paul Claudel, and switch gracefully to
Christian Dior. Strangers should glance at photographs of Mistinguett, Maurice Rostand, the Dutch
painter Van Dongen, and such celebrities before
attending first nights. Then they may be sure of
recognizing them in the flesh.

The approved supper places for after-theatre are
Weber's, Fouquet's, the Café du Rondpoint, and
Chez Francis. Inclusion of the last-named café and
restaurant, in an official French document after liberation, was intended to convey that, in spite of
the fact that for several years before World War
II, some waiters of that famous Alsatian restaurant
in the Place de l'Alma were active Nazi spies, and
that immediately on German occupation the place
was turned over, lock, stock and barrel, to S.S. offi-

cers and Nazi bigwigs, the traditions and significance of the establishment, as a musicians' and composers' hangout, were too valuable to discard. Collaborators in connection with that and other public places of refreshment and rendezvous have mostly been dealt with, most of them shot.

The "birthday book" makes no reference to war or factions, but the fact that the pocketbooks of the rich *mondains* have outstripped their appetites is wistfully regretted. The "serious" after-theatre supper has degenerated into a mere snack, because modern men, for one reason or another, in France as elsewhere, and with notable exceptions like White Russians, cannot eat, drink or digest like the giants of old.

What other publicists, in describing what a capital city has to offer, would choose, as did the French, a first-night rally of literary and musical politicians and the organization of world enthusiasm, followed by opportunities in designated dining rooms and on certain *terrasses* to overhear brilliant exchanges of opinion as to the merits of a given piece?

Other attractions played up in the book included the Opera and Ballet, the Circuses (*d'Hiver* and *Médrano*), charity balls like the *Bal des Petits Lits Blancs*, a benefit for ailing French children, the *Gala de l'Union des Artistes*, the *Bal de la Violette*, and a dinner dance in the Golf Club at St. Cloud.

The mention of charity affairs brings to mind an American couple who previous to and during World War I, and the period between great wars, were as much in the French public eye as any foreigners are likely to be. I refer to the late Mr. and Mrs. E. Berry Wall. Who knows how well the Berry Walls understood the French, or anything else beyond sports and society? It is certain, however, that the French loved and admired the Berry Walls, and so did the Paris reporters. For one thing, while other Mr. and Mrs. combinations shifted like colored tabs in a kaleidoscope, marrying, divorcing, exchanging, remarrying, separating and quibbling, Mr. and Mrs. E. Berry Wall remained steadfast and true, quite touchingly fond of each other. French propaganda for tourism and national income from Americans was not as highly organized in pre-War II days as it is now. But there were contacts. Mrs. E. Berry Wall, for instance, was in perpetual charge of a fund established largely by Americans to provide milk for needy French children. She would stop at nothing within the limits of good taste to get contributions from those who could afford them in a big way.

Society painters, for instance, who flocked to Paris and got huge fees for doing bad portraits and memorials while talented artists starved, were targets for Mrs. E. Berry Wall. She fixed it with the management of the Luxembourg Museum (now mercifully extinct) to buy paintings by any painter who had coughed up a couple of thousand dollars for Mrs. Wall's pet milk fund. The obedient French press would publish little items to the effect that a work by Hiram Haskins, the famous American painter from Philadelphia or Oklahoma, had been purchased for the national French museum in the Luxembourg Gardens. The newspaper never disclosed that the painting in question, having been bought for less than a song, was tossed into a basement heap under the galleries, never to be brought above stairs again. And it was not stressed that on the list of milk-fund contributors, Maître Haskins had entered his name, to the tune of ten thousand dollars.

The French are capable of almost any kind of graft or hokus-pokus, but they finagle very graciously, and with no hypocritical unction or self-deception.

France is shaped somewhat like a magnolia blossom in process of opening. There are six fairly well-defined points and the diversity of the activities and population contained in this comparatively small country strikes one forcibly as one enumerates the tips of the magnolia petals. Starting farthest north are the mining and industrial provinces, bordering on Belgium, where the life of the worker is hard, the air is sooty and grimy, and a situation verging on industrial rebellion perpetually exists. Moving clockwise, to the next point (thus passing over the province of Champagne), we find Alsace and Lorraine, with French and German traditions and loyalties so badly mixed that the members of families seated at table often have no common language.

Continue through the Franche-Comté and a corner of Burgundy, through Savoy and the Dauphiné, and you find yourself in sunny Provence, a world of sloth and romance that always had and still has unearthly qualities, and a fabulous, tough waterfront.

Traverse Languedoc and stretching from point to point, touching on the east the wine-dark sea of Homer and on the west the turbulent Atlantic, the province of the Pyrenees runs the length of the Spanish border.

Cross Guyenne and Gascony, and the group of provinces of the west, and there are Brittany and Normandy, side by side and as different as Eire and England.

That leaves, as the central core of France, the Ile de France, Maine, the Loire Valley, the middle provinces, Limousin and Marche, Auvergne and Lyons.

What a wealth of history, anthropology, geology and humanity. In truth, if you think of France provincially, the unity you have felt and expounded seems to break like an ice floe in spring. But does it? These provinces, corresponding superficially to the states of America and the counties of Great Britain, have cultural distinction within the national hegemony which, in each instance, has had to be imposed and maintained from without.

Again my instinct prompts me to start farthest

north. Certainly the Author of our Days did not cause all those little compass needles to point toward Polaris unless He attached much significance that way. Shall we praise Dunkirk? A moment of silence. Calais, which seasick voyagers have spied from their rail of woe so many times and oft? Boulogne, where fishwives have their annual cursing and invective contest? Or shall we ease eastward, way over to Valenciennes, where lace comes from?

I can never think of Valenciennes without remembering Watteau, who died there in his thirties of an illness which had restricted much of his life but probably served to fire his genius with fever. It is surprising what one or two degrees Fahrenheit will do for an artist. Watteau, in his early twenties, fell madly in love with a dancer at the Paris Opera, who was many years older than the painter. He had won no kudos in his teens, was poor, sick and unprepossessing. This dancer gave him a runaround throughout the years that one would not wish on a type like Tiberius or Goering, but the dirtiest trick of all she reserved for the last. After she had shot her bolt and he had gained fame and an income, she married him. He was still mad about her, and the resultant exertion, inevitable in such cases, finished the first painter of France, the man with such originality and vision that he could not be content with flat colors, mixed like dough on a palette, but put them on the canvas in separate brush strokes, to be combined and blended by the spectator's eye. How can we thank him for that innovation which in a sense makes collaborating painters of the simplest of us? I still contend that Watteau lasted long enough to have an affair with his sister-in-law, thus cuckolding his wife, who was a real champion in that field.

Arras, Amiens and St. Quentin strike chords, minor chords with slow drumbeat, in the heart of many, many English parents who still remember World War I and that "thin red line." Those who care for churches will speak of St. Omer and Abbeville.

But the provinces of the North are notable today for France's heavy industries, and everyone who knows his own country is aware that heavy industry imposes a dignity on a region that is also a pall, while man persists in his inhumanity to man. And in Northern France, man does persist. And so do the workers. When abused too much, they fight, and the soldiers take pot shots at them. Some live to lose a strike and work again, too many hours, in too dangerous places. Some die, and few are the monuments raised to them, as yet. The Frenchman, descendant of the anarchistic Gaul, cannot be pushed around with impunity. The employer, descendant of the Roman conqueror, retains his fondness for one-way laws, stressing property rights above all others. The descendant of the Frank, with his community spirit, tries to organize unions, and he does. The French believe, to a man, that some solution will apply itself to labor strife, although few of them can agree on a program. They turn out radicals who inspire the maximum in fear and dread, because the deeds they do live after them. They breed conservatives so far to the right that they accept feudal doctrines as gospel, and believe they are upholding eternal values as their bank accounts mount. In the middle is your average Frenchman, and the way he turns, in any given year, is that year's policy of France.

Rudyard Kipling, whom France recognizes as the No. 1 English *fumiste* (windbag) with a genuine talent far beyond his own mental grasp, had this to say of the Champagne country. (We are moving around clockwise, again.)

"Whither the dappled Argonne, the cloud-shadow-
ing packing
  Either horizon with ghosts; or exquisite, carven
  Villages hewn from the cliff, the torrents behind
    them
  Feeding their never quenched lights . . . .
      It is enough—it is France."

The Province of Champagne yields sparkling wine, contented woolly sheep with almost no brains and battlefields where some battles were lost and a few were won. It was formerly, before manure was esteemed and utilized, and oak forests had burned and given way to pine and birches, a barren region. Yves Gandon has called it "an ocean of chalk." To me it is one of the beauty areas, because I went there as a soldier and it was my first war and my first province of France. I entered France, one might say, through the department of the Haute Marne, and I would not have chosen another.

Chaumont was general headquarters for the first A.E.F. In St. Dizier a printing plant, the second to be authorized and approved by the King, one of my favorite kings, François I, was haunted each month in the late twenties by Eugene Jolas and me, when we were enjoying our adventure, an international magazine called *transition*. St. Menehould is where, of all spots on this planet, folks understand most about grilling pigs' feet. Rheims is a *cause célèbre*. Troyes is where French is spoken as German is spoken in Hanover. Of that region, so steeped in wine tradition and war memories and all that is historic, in regions where the Hun and the Gaul still clash, I wish to call attention to the old walled city of Langres, just a comfortable few hours' journey from Paris, to the east, by train or by car. Tourists, starved for what is genuine and quaint, have thus far passed it by. I never met a tourist there.

The old city, and there is no other, covers the top of a hill, one of the foothills of the Vosges. The wall still stands, and one may walk on top of it, around the city, and on the outside is the fertile plain, those white roads lined with poplars, on hill-tops, red-roofed villages set off with stately trees, surrounded by farms that make patchworks of color in concentric bands. Inside the city you will find the Middle Ages you have heard so much about, and you will learn that they had something we have lost and lacked much we have discovered. There is nothing else remarkable about Langres, few relics in museums which bring pilgrims thence, no restaurants whose specialities are watchwords of gourmets. The food is excellent and plain, and not expensive enough to be frenziedly praised. You will tread stones that were old when Columbus sailed the seas, if you care for treading old stones. You will look into windows out of which the age of chivalry has passed, leaving behind its aroma and flavor. You will feel the ache of wondering, of what was the past, of what is now, and what, if anything, shall be. You will not be talkative on the way back toward Paris, and home.

There is a slang expression, as crude as it is effec-tive, used in connection with such conflicting emotions as surprise, good health, quick resentment, rush of adrenalin or embarrassment. "Was *his* face red!" one will ejaculate. He whose face is red most likely, if he is a Frenchman, will be from Burgundy, where the wine is red, and should not be looked down upon, according to the Scriptures, because looking down on wine in the glass precludes or interferes with drinking it. Where there is wine there is also music, and the Dukes of Burgundy, in their day, were great patrons of that art.

Today we must not forget that, alongside the wine slopes, are deposits of coal and ore, and that Burgundy bears its share of heavy industry. Also Dijon, its capital, is one of the most delightful university cities in the world, and has a restaurant called *Les Quatres Faisans* (The Four Pheasants) that is worth a trip to Europe from almost anywhere. And Belley on the lower tip of Burgundy, we have already mentioned.

And so to Lorraine and Alsace, with capitals, Nancy and Strasbourg. Because Strasbourg, with its wealth of interests, commercial, diplomatic, cultural and larcenous, has been echoed all through song and story, and the real history of Lorraine has been obscured by so much cosmic nonsense about Joan of Arc, I prefer to dwell on that land of the Moselle and its university city, Nancy, hardly second to Dijon in scholastic weight, while it is infinitely more beautiful.

The art museum at Nancy has a quality of its own, because the footage devoted to the stuffed shirts of French painting like Rigaud and Vernet is rather less than the tourist will find elsewhere. I do not wish to make it appear difficult to understand the French. I want to show that it is not only worth-while, but essential for a well-rounded modern man to have some standard of appraisal of his cultural leaders. Whoever is blind to or ignorant of French painting, all the way from Clouet and Fouquet to Matisse and Picasso, will have to learn French evolution the hard way. Perhaps it can be done. But why handicap oneself? The world is rich in good reproductions, and readers have eyes.

It was a native of Lorraine, inspired by a Norman, Nicolas Poussin, in Rome, who "let daylight into painting." Previously it had been a noble but rather dismal achievement. Claude Lorrain, *né* Claude Gelée, braved the sunlight, forsaking the dimness of cloisters and draped studios. Once a corner like that is rounded, in art, there is no turning back. Besides works by Claude, the Nancy museum has "Autumn," one of the finest Manets, and fine examples of Delacroix.

The natives of East Lorraine had to be given over, bodily, in 1870, with their beloved land, to be fitted, like Procrustes of old, to a heavy German sickbed. The proof of their stamina is that they survived, as Frenchmen and Frenchwomen, to be liberated by the compromising treaty of Versailles. A plague on all the ranters who would forbid civilization to use surgery on its cancers.

"Tell me what you eat and I will tell you what you are," is still a sound proverb in France. Alsatian cooking and Alsatian wines, because its hosts and merchants have the gift of amplification, and apply it so deftly to propaganda, are renowned wherever food and drink are important. The Lorraine cuisine, less ponderous, may be praised without raising the voice. It has all the charm of the countryman's fare, as Doré Ogrizek says. Lorrainians dote on *pâté*. They make a hotpot of vegetables and native sausage with fresh *and* salted bacon that sounds chords of a gastronomic hymn. The Lorrainian cream sauces of fresh cream and egg yolks inspired Rossini to create his famous variations of white sauces, and put on kilos of weight, which, modern fanatics to the contrary, is as helpful to man's spirit as it may be burdensome to faint hearts, vain athletes or actors who have to work full time at sex appeal (while seldom developing it to any great extent), and conspirators who have to slink through narrow rifts between walls.

Our guiding clock hands creep over the map of France to the province known as Franche-Comté, where grandeur and beauty make a most effective compromise. Listen to the sensitive Frenchman of the Roman and Frank persuasion, Charles Nodier:

The Jura mountain range does not share with the Alps the imposing but melancholy privilege of eternal snow. The lakes stretching at its feet have not the immensity of those of Switzerland (which could be splashed into the American Great Lakes without affecting the level perceptibly), nor even of the Scottish lochs. But they are perhaps more pleasing in their less extensive dimensions and in our experience they evoke thoughts of the tenderest and most homely character. It is as if their very limited bounds were better adapted to human sentiment and personal affection.

The Frenchmen of the Franche-Comté, having alternately been warriors, and/or rude peasants and stubborn artisans, have had much less time for amusement than most Frenchmen in a less controversial region. Nevertheless, the men did some of the best wood carving in Europe for their homes, and the women spent long evenings making rustic embroidery that reached the plane of high art. That meant an easy period for the generations coming just before World War I, and between Wars I and II, since the younger people could reap a rich harvest selling antiques fashioned by the toil of their forebears. The Franche-Comté thus has been stripped of its most beautiful objects indoors, while retaining its landscape in a form almost ideal.

The French have strong sentiment for conserving national treasures of art, utility and invention, but the individual Frenchman has an urge to trade that is almost an obsession, like the gambling fever or the craving of an habitué for narcotics. He would not sell his grandmother if she chanced to be sympathetic, but grandmothers frequently are antagonistic, and in that case would be sold, if a buyer showed the color of French, American, Swiss, Belgian or Swedish money, i.e., the kinds of money Frenchmen of that eastern region are sure about.

The outside interest in the Franche-Comté seems to have centered lately (in the last hundred years) around Besançon, one of the foremost French cities whose name has that cedilla under the "c," to soften it, as in *garçon*, and not leave it hard as in Macon, the best cheap red wine, and a community in Georgia, U.S.A.

The first item, however, to ask for in the Franche-Comté would be crayfish, with kirsch (distilled from cherry stones) for an appetizer, and a dry white wine, a Poligny, for instance, to wash them down. Then buy a local briar pipe, for a hundred francs or so, and whistle "*La Marseillaise*," written by Rouget de Lisle who was born at Lons, and wrote the piece originally as a "Song of the Rhine Army." Never mind, you patriotic French who think your song sprung up spontaneously with the French Revolution. America's "Star-Spangled Banner" crashed the sound waves first as an English drinking song called "Anacreon in Heaven."

When someone asked the great Professor Copeland of Harvard who was the "greatest" French poet, "Copey" replied, "Alas, Victor Hugo." Alas, Victor Hugo was born in the Franche-Comté, near Besançon, because his father, then a captain, chanced to be garrisoned in that neighborhood.

The humorist, Tristan Bernard, was born of a Jewish family of horse dealers. Bernard's Jewish ancestors made the family solid with the aristocracy by hiding, saving and protecting the nearest Marquis and his loved ones during the Terror.

Courbet, the painter who made peasants an acceptable painting subject, instead of Greek gods, goddesses, mythological characters, saints and lords and ladies, worked near Besançon.

Trout fishermen in the Franche-Comté will more than break even.

On to Savoy and the Dauphiné. The St. Bernard dogs with brandy strapped to their chests, who pause at the summit of a rise along the Alps, if they are facing west, look down upon Savoy and the Dauphiné. They could hardly do better, and easily do worse.

I am not given to the slow form of suicide known as "living in the past," an affliction, a kind of madness that prompts its victims not only to impossibilize themselves but negate the age which proves too much for them. In Chambéry, the highland city which has outgrown a long series of modernities; in Chamonix, where ancient heroes fought dragons and men of today pit themselves against nature and physics for their sports; in Aix and Evian, where water, hot and cold, prevails over milk and honey, wine and women, snow and ice; at Grenoble, the king of campuses; through the Alpine passes; in the valleys; on the peaks; the visitors, the invaders, the natives, the defenders are timeless, like their vistas, their occupations, their absent historical compatriots, their liberties, their laws.

Who can feel, as dead men, as corpses embalmed and planted, Hector Berlioz, Stendhal (Henri Beyle), Jean-Jacques Rousseau, François de Sales, Fantin-Latour, Bayard, Berthollet. They inhabit Savoy and the Dauphiné; their thoughts were their valid acts, their compulsions, their contributions. Consider the No. 1 French composer of music, without whom France would never have her due: Berlioz, whose romance with Henrietta Simpson,

great English Shakespearean actress, is the model
for those of whom it can truly be said, "They lived
unhappily forever after"—Berlioz, whose great res-
urrection mass is in music what Michelangelo's ceiling of the Sistine Chapel is to painting.

In the meanest, most corrupt newspaper, published anywhere no matter what date, one finds
proof that chivalry is not dead, that chivalry cannot die. Who symbolized it for all time? Bayard
of Savoy.

The psychological novel, as opposed to empty
stories of "action," has always been for the élite,
and from them sways the mob which thinks it cares
nothing for what influences it the most. Stendhal
was the master, when he lived and worked at St.
Marcellin. He is master today. His *Charterhouse of
Parma* and *The Red and the Black* top the fiction
list, while his *Memoirs* tower above the vales of
autobiography as the Alps dominate his native
province. One of the few things for which Napoleon the Great may be praised is that Stendhal
followed and admired him. We cannot throw
away even a tyrant whom Stendhal found worthy
of his admiration.

There was a group of great Frenchmen, painters,
poets, and prophets, known as the Impressionists.
To whom must we be thankful today that we can
step into the *Musée des Indépendents,* in the
Tuileries, in Paris, and find in the reception room,

life size, garbed in the conventional black, Verlaine, Rimbaud, Baudelaire, Monet, Manet, Pissarro, Sisley, Toulouse-Lautrec and their companions? A painter from the Savoy, on the outskirts of Grenoble, named Fantin-Latour. With the patience of a saint and the skill of a demon, he did group portraits, as meticulous with clothes as with substance, presence and appearance.

Social consciousness, independence of spirit, kinship with nature, all got their impetus from Jean-Jacques Rousseau, one of the few men who has had courage to "confess." Is it a matter for discouragement that a man with a vast mind and a duty to share it can be reduced by circumstances and prevailing prejudices to abandoning his bastard children in infancy? Was Berlioz a cad and Rousseau a coward? Was Napoleon, now all is said and done, just a brute who broke the heart of Josephine? Was Jesus taking any chances when he invited whoever was without sin to throw stones at one who had been caught?

How strange it is that when I try to describe twin provinces, which have all there is of majesty and natural spectacular beauty, I stray into the realm of the mind and cannot extricate myself!

The French in the Savoy climb mountains, descend on skis, drink Evian, bathe in hot springs and traverse the seven ages of man. They understand that outsiders, with money, will pay for relief and entertainment, for scenery and exercise, for glancing at memorials, scanning guidebooks, for food and beds and conversation. They raise sheep, tobacco, grain and nuts. In a country that worships its trees to a deeper extent than did the Druids or the Gauls, the Savoy and the Dauphiné have the oldest, staunchest chestnuts, evergreens, beeches and larches.

Toward the middle of the fourteenth century, Humbert II, founder of the University of Grenoble, deeded his two provinces to the King of France, on condition that the Sovereign's eldest son should henceforth bear the title of Dauphin and that Savoy and Dauphiné should continue to live under Humbert's laws. This last-named prerogative was defended successfully by the Savoyards until, at the time of the first Revolution, they agreed voluntarily to pay taxes and obey the laws of the Republic.

It was at Laffrey that Napoleon, arriving from the island of Elba on March 7, 1815, with ready wisecracks and his little cocked hat, won over the soldiers who had been sent to arrest him and continued his march to Paris, then to Waterloo.

Now we go over the divide, and off the deep end —from the cool regions of the north, through the bubbles of the Champagne, the kraut of Alsace, the trout streams of the Franche-Comté, around the rim of the half-blown magnolia, the map of France. We have skirted the Alps of Savoy, with its worldly-wise hillbillies and mountaineers who, less than one hundred years ago, conducted their town-council meetings in Latin. We are now about to enter Provence. To a Northerner of any land, it would seem impossible that such a region could exist and support inhabitants, or that inhabitants would match any such region and feel, not only content, but a feline detachment and superiority to the rest of France. For that matter, the Provence folk, if they are aware that anything out of Europe exists at all, feel superior to whatever it is, on principle.

Provence did not want to be joined forcibly to Northern France, but today, aware that the only alternative to being Frenchmen would be to find themselves Macaronis (Italians), they accept the lesser, by far, of two evils and shrug off the consequences, which operate both ways.

Writers, like Hilaire Belloc, Ford Madox Ford, Donald Peatty, Sisley Huddleston, James Pope Hennessy, Gonzague Truc and Ezra Pound, have all begun to fizz and spume whenever they tried writing about Provence, the land of the dread wind, mistral; of silver olive trees and rich olive oil, wild garlic and wild thyme, and a monotonous, vindictive sun.

Still, I see my duty and cannot evade it. Provence must be dealt with in a book about the French, if for no other reason than its speech, much more than a dialect because it perpetuates the music of old French and brings pastel tones into happy drowsiness. But I do not mean to include the seacoast which borders it around the Mediterranean, from Garavan, Menton, Monaco, Nice and Cannes, around through St. Tropez, the Hyères isles, Toulon, Marseilles, Martigues and les Sts. Maries. The true Provençal, safely inland, although only a few miles, pays no attention to the coast, its solid citizens, its riffraff, or to any maritime affairs. The Provençaux deplore the coast and whatever leaks through it to their towns and barren spaces.

The Alps dribble into the northeast corner of Provence but the highlanders of that region belong with the Savoyards, and not with Provence of the mistral and shimmering sky, red earth and dull slate vegetation, hens roosting in cactus, vultures wheeling on high. It is no fault of the natives that communities like Arles and Avignon have become notorious, because of Van Gogh and Cézanne, stray Popes and children's songs. Neither have any of the natives read the reactions of Smollett, Mérimée, Stendhal, Dickens, Canon Kingsley, Mrs. Browning (perish the thought!), Lady Blessington or J. A. Symonds. Nor did anybody from Arles collaborate with Bizet in his opera called *L'Arlésienne*, which is contained in every collection of incidental music for the silent movies, to be used in connection with orgies on the screen.

It is lucky for Arles that Vincent Van Gogh's religion was of the hard-shelled Protestant kind. Had he been a Catholic, and sainted for his work, I am positive that several dozen human ears would have been dug up by this time, to serve as holy relics. The folks of Arles would not care.

Lady Blessington once lunched in a "large crazy old mansion" which served Arles as an hotel, and found it noteworthy that, as the children spread the word around town, natives gathered to peep discreetly, then stare openly, at the strangers. Nothing is more characteristic of Provençaux, Catalans, or the related Balearic Islanders. Their ancestors always have been curious about strangers, and suspicious of them, more often than not with full justification. The Catholicism of Provence is closer to that of Catalonia and Spain than to freethinking Northern France. It is hard and knotty, like ancient grapevine stalks, taken straight by the women and openly ridiculed by most of the men.

Provençaux who have not died long ago from wind madness, caused by continuous flapping of skirts and all flexible objects and the tendency to crook one's neck seaward for days and nights at a time, accept the mistral, sired by the fourth assistant devil, Panzouzou, as a reason for women to behave capriciously and shrewishly, and for men to loaf and get drunk. Wormwood grows wild, respect for Northern laws runs low, so absinthe is the summer drink, and rum or brandy keeps body and soul together during the rainy season.

The natives are stingy with non-relatives, cunning in petty affairs, secretive about trifles, but in the end prove too lazy and essentially good-natured to be troublesome. If they distrust visitors, they also distrust one another. Henry James sent swarms of tourists like locusts over Provence by gushing about Roman ruins, but there are six times as many in Tuscany, where the landscape is less desperate and the folks more expansive.

Gertrude Stein did Provence more good than James or Dickens did. She warned all hands that "If you go to Provence you'll find you're getting nervous down there. You'll find yourself having a big fight with your best friend. You just can't help it." Gertrude was referring to Provence when a mistral was blowing. She found it quaint and tolerable at other times.

Natives of Provence, however they suffer, grin and mutter with satisfaction when a mistral is blowing hard, knowing that their baked plains give it a chance to gather force for the dudes and low-lifes along the coast, especially the Riviera.

Good Catholics will shun Avignon and the old papal palace because it was there that Pope Benedict reigned for years after having been officially ousted by the Roman rivals. There are special types of people who will stand on the bridge and pay predatory kiddies to dance and sing that insipid song *"Sur le pont d'Avignon."* Such types will be marked to be cheated, overcharged, shortchanged and cajoled. If they ask directions for motoring they will wind up somewhere far from their goal—and be just as well off.

Mirabeau, who is still scorned by the pseudo-aristocrats and tatters of nobility because of his democratic sentiments, is shrugged off by avid Republicans on account of his wistful attachment to the person of Marie Antoinette, along with Lafayette, and others. He was of the stubborn, equivocal temperament characteristic of men of Central Provence. Cézanne, who has spread the region's beauty to all corners of the earth, there to repose till the end of time, worked in the zone between parched inland Provence and the ribbon refreshed by the scent of the wine-dark sea, the snot-green sea, and the rich widows and unattached women on the loose who infest the Riviera and usually get what is coming to them, with compound interest, in the person of a tall White Russian, glib Hungarian, English remittance chap, or a tough Frenchman of the Jean Gabin, Jean-Pierre Aumont, or Maurice Chevalier class.

We cannot pass over Fragonard, who saw the

light at Grasse, behind Cannes. This meticulous French painter, who spent weeks putting on canvas the result of an instantaneous glance at his model, had the unworldliness and detachment of his Provence neighbors. He remained narrow, intense, cantankerous and inspired wherever he found himself. In Paris he enjoyed such vogue with boudoir scenes in which he never participated that Louis XVI gave him an ample suite of rooms in the Louvre Palace (now the Museum to end Museums). Fragonard lived in the King's palace like a provincial, and when the Revolution broke over the heads of everyone, the painter from Provence stayed on in royal halls until rescued by David. Then he lived his old age in bewildered seclusion. He could not change his style, or use it for patriotic subjects, which, for reasons he did not grasp at all, had become *de rigueur*.

The political fox and schemer, Thiers, lived on the outskirts of Marseilles, where people never tell the truth if a lie will serve one-sixteenth as well. And within a couple of miles of him was Daumier, who drew and painted the truth like no one before or since.

Toulon is the principal French naval base, although the French Navy today is only the shell of a fighting or policing force. The people of Toulon, and the national authorities in Paris, seem reluctant to repair the war scars, or to clear and use the waterfront again. Few Frenchmen are sure whether the commanders who gave orders to blow up France's great battleships and accessory men-of-war were knavish poltroons "too proud to fight," whether the admirals were too afraid of the Communist seamen to risk an engagement, or whether certain complicated reasons will develop when history is written, indicating that the abject destruction of the fleet was necessary, therefore right.

Everyone knows about Marseilles, even if they do not credit the full vigor and depravity of one of the toughest seaports in the world, and one that has not become milder as elsewhere civilization mellows. Some pious chumps have torn down a few old walls in the red-light district and put up plaster flats. No woman missed a trick and no roistering sailor pined for satisfaction in the course of the stupid reconstruction.

Mistral, still the great poet of the South of France, or Provence at least, did so much for the French language that the moderns from the region, Jean Aicard and Edmond Rostand, both could be spared. The other modern Provence writer, Charles Maurras, a bigot in philosophy, an arch-reactionary in politics, one of the century's prime haters of democracy and general education, and a scoundrel and hypocrite in his social and family life, will serve as a horrible ingrown example of the Provence mentality at its meanest and worst.

At its best, the spirit of Provence, maritime-wise, was exemplified by Admiral Pierre-André Suffren, whose naval tactics in various engagements off the American coast during the Revolution, at Gibraltar with the Allied fleet, and in the East Indian waters, were devious and obstinate, like the minds of his countrymen.

Provence will not be remembered as vividly for its famous sons, or its backward people, as for its pastel shades of landscape and the scent of wild thyme, the scorching sun, the maddening wind, the hot bleak sky, the chill when it rains, and the speech, which is better than pure music, since it is impure music.

Provence, by sharp contrast with the mountain states of the Franche-Comté and the world's well-spring of wine and high living which Burgundy typifies, prepares one who would understand the French without trying to be a stage Frenchman himself, or a Madame Pompadour herself, for Languedoc and its surrounding areas in Guyenne and Gascony, and up as far as Limousin.

When a healthy, worldly man thinks of love, or the ambience of amour, or the shape of the woman who may descend from the cloud of unexpectedness or step toward him through the mist of frustration, bare and frank, or seductively clothed and congen-

itally prepared—when a virile man allows himself
to think a dream may become fragrant, tactile and
real, for twenty minutes, or decades, he accepts a
vision of a Frenchwoman he may or may not have
met, or a woman from another land who, unlike
her compatriots, is just as alluring in an acquired
French manner. Languedoc and the vicinity in the
south of France becomes the origin of his urge and
emotion and chance of fulfilment, whether he
knows it or not.

The people of Languedoc, who spoke Provençal,
and fought to the death to avoid becoming French
—that is, stern, religiously fanatic and king-sub-
servient Northern French of the twelfth and thir-
teenth centuries—had the distinction of weaving
the magic of romance about the miracle of love,
which had been a hit-or-miss, or devil-take-the-hind-
most procedure, through the days of Egypt, Greece
and Rome—the early Christian days and what have
been misnamed the "Dark Ages."

No age in that enchanted section of France has
been dark. Tragic, yes. The best men were mas-
sacred by zealots of the Church in the Albigensian
"crusade." Enough to fill a library has been written
of that, and most of it from a hypocritical ecclesiastical or official angle. The troubadours, and their
courts of love? There are volumes devoted to them,
and none completely satisfactory. Because the types
who have chosen to perpetuate the troubadours'

memories have been unvigorous by nature, over-delicate by literary or commercial or social instinct. Dr. Kinsey was born far too late.

Will it be possible to override the barren impression that Languedoc, as contrasted with Rome at the peak of licentiousness, was pale, and that knights and their lady loves were content with absent treatment, and thrilled to the shadow without the substance? Those men of the South of France, and the women they taught and who conferred on them the higher degrees in return, added to the spice and zest of amour, instead of diluting it. Where violence, brutality and sadism had produced the usual results of fatigue and disgust, the knights and yeomen, the pages and squires, and all hands but the dour clergy, proceeded in the other direction. Tenderness, talk, song, literature were only the vaporous emanations of the piquant intrigue and furious frolic. No one would claim that, since knights were addicted to journeying (the vibrant loved ones left temporarily behind) they did not find solace along the wayside with stray females and other gentlemen on quests, with variations.

The champions of love, the men and women who were gobbled by a tyrannical faction, in being nationalized, transformed the Northerners into the most resourceful, liberal, accomplished and life-loving people of the modern world; those French we are anxious to understand. Seven and one-half centuries have accomplished the blend, so that to-day the provinces of France, divergent as they are, have all the essentials in common and are Frenchmen, first, and provincials in a preparatory or secondary way.

The joint and mutual manifestation of love, refined, cultivated, invigorated, restrained, crescendoed, let run wild, got its best lasting impetus from the martyrs and survivors of Languedoc and Limousin.

The knights sang about love sadly, that is, the songs were sad, not they. They overlooked no bouncing bets, and used force on busybodies, bounders or rivals, not on the ladies who could shiver and sigh, and had to help in divesting themselves, sooner or later, but not too late. The troubadours reversed the mocking Roman proverb which held that a man should boast while taking off his armor, rather than when he was putting it on.

To those ladies, and serving wenches of Southern France, who played their parts with such grace and gusto, all women of the roguish kind, the very best of women anywhere, any time, must acknowledge a debt of sound example. Nell Gwyn and Moll Flanders, centuries later, would have been their comrades and co-conspirators, not sublime exceptions to a humdrum flock.

A cursory glance through French history indicates that French leaders, worthy or detestable, were much more adept at using the Vatican's political, military or superstitional organizations and forces for national purposes than submitting to religious unity, or unification which meant the end of France. The French, especially under Louis XIV, the king most extravagantly touted, suppressed local Protestants with a cruelty, brutality and thoroughness which, of all the national characteristics, are now the least conspicuous and the hardest to admit or grasp. There is scarcely a country in Europe (one does not count Franco Spain as a country but a neglected infection the Western world stupidly persists in leaving untreated) so devoid of Protestant churches and churchmen as France.

In France, the Protestant element having been diminished by scheming kings not long before our era of republicanism and democracy, there is a sound fifty per cent of men and women whose minds are uncluttered by any brand of mystic belief (with expensive organization and elaborate trappings) and who are as near to freethinkers as we have. If freedom wins, as we must assume it will, we shall have those lucid French to thank. Not that the British and the North Americans will not have made material, political and humane contributions. The French have led the battle in the sphere of the mind.

Languedoc gave us Toulouse-Lautrec, the martyred Jean Jaurès, also Alphonse Daudet. The internally turbulent and outwardly hospitable Toulouse has universalized the *cassoulet* of goose and white beans. The traveler pauses at Villefranche, Carcassonne, Montpellier, Nîmes and northward at Tournon and Le Puy.

We have only to step over the border into the related Guyenne and Gascogne for historical, cultural and gastronomical sources, including the country seat of Henry IV at Pau, the birthplaces of Gautier, the late Marshal Foch and Ingres, who painted harem women in terms of ivory, alabaster and cool flesh. The region that produces the world's best liqueur brandy is Armagnac. The small fields where the choicest truffles grow are near Perigueux. White wine and all the clarets come from the wine-growing slopes around Bordeaux. Bayonne is a barren border city where, however, the top swindler of his time, one Stavisky, got his start in the local municipal pawnshop. And the descendants of those living farther inland devised Roquefort cheese.

The ports of the world have their denizens and amateurs and their places in the memories of men who, since the Phœnicians, have gone down to the seas in ships. Bordeaux is as lively as any, without being vulgarly lurid or self-consciously low. The poor miss few tricks, and seldom do they groan. The prosperous middle-class merchants toss their pots in approved carousing places. The rich, and very few are too rich for human comfort, try to keep within the graces of all others, are generous with women and appreciative of wine. There are not many important seaport cities which have such a comparatively low percentage of stuffed shirts among the important citizens. Frenchwomen of the middle class, the wives and mothers, Church supporters, the wearers of deceptively unattractive clothes, who speak carefully, according to the schoolbook, a compromise between parochial elocution and the *Théâtre Français*, the kind who dote on coaching and correcting their well-behaved children in public, find, all over France, that respectability, like virtue, is its own and only reward. Free acknowledgments are due, at this point, to the witty Oscar Wilde, whose best phrases are too fundamental and far-reaching to be filed and not applied. But getting back to that respectable Frenchwoman, who does everything so properly, it is just as well, on the whole, that one seldom gets well enough acquainted to "understand" her. When a man does, he is all too likely to find he has a tiger by the tail who has contrived to make herself radio-active, into the bargain.

I detest generalities, and so do the French. Nevertheless, it is safe to state that any female born and raised in European France has emotional, devotional and passionate potentialities which, if unaroused, are explosively cumulative and, if active and contained, may distract the most prudent male from righting wrongs, increasing the store of human knowledge, oiling the wheels of commerce or prosperity, diffusing art for art's sake, or saving for a rainy day.

The Frenchman in comfortable circumstances, who keeps up a front, respectable or unpretentious, is not oversuccessful, as a lover, outside the sphere of his normal experience. He is too delicate for a foreign female dunce, and too direct and reasonable for the borderline adventuress who goes to France believing that twenty million Frenchmen must be Maurice Chevaliers. With women on the loose, or receptive, from the United States, French gallants find rougher going than Italians, for instance. The Frenchman can utter a fair amount of nonsense, but his native sense of restraint stops him where the Italian flesh-hound would begin. The Frenchman from Bordeaux, where gossip spreads like radio waves, would be discreet near home and go unencumbered to Paris.

Discretion and kindness are synonymous with the active French. What we call "the double standard" is with them plain common sense. A French

husband or wife, as long as they respected each
other and wished to continue the arrangement,
would protect each other from disturbing knowledge or cause for suspicion as carefully as they
would shield each other from cholera or tetanus
germs. If the man is caught or compromised, most
realistic wives in France would forgive him. Crimes
of passion, so-called, are given special and separate
consideration in French courts. Attractive or presentable women are seldom convicted. Men who
have shed blood in fits of jealous anger are dealt
with leniently.

The punishment is designed not only to fit the
crime but the provocation, and that human frailty
which, with believers and non-believers, is an article of faith. A French court of law, either in the
city or in the country, gives an Anglo-Saxon the
impression of a non-musical comedy tangled hope-
lessly in red tape (faded); the informality in tense
moments being equaled only by the absurd and
finicky preoccupation with paper details when the
cause is trivial. Nevertheless, were I on trial with
anything to present on my side of a case, I would
rather take a chance in a French court than before
a tribunal in any other land. Why? Because after
all the gobbledegook, the inkpot throwing, name-
calling, and disorderly conduct is over, the judge,
or judges, or judges and jury, come up with a de-

cision which is as refreshingly just and sensible, balanced and equitable, as Solomon in his most judicial moments could have achieved.

The foreign summer visitors who spend a few weeks on the shore of Brittany will meet the Celtic Bretons in their villages and coves and find them much as they were many centuries ago. They suffer from a kind of Christianity as near superstition as religion can get, these days, and one of the hardiest and most dangerous means of livelihood, which at best or worst is a gamble, that is, fishing and combing the rugged littoral. These crusty Bretons will not be speaking French, as a rule, but regional Celtic dialects imperfectly understood by other Bretons a few miles away. For summer folks, on whom they are dependent for some of their meager income, they will provide clean rooms and superb food, of which the shellfish and sea-fish elements, with their life-giving phosphorous and iodine, predominate. They will smile when it seems appropriate, make the minimum of one-way conversation, but enough to serve as welcome. They will not stare at foreign females in modern bathing suits on beaches, or have them arrested, as the Spanish provincials might. They care not, as long as their guests pay promptly, who sleeps with whom in any style. The shore Bretons, fanatically pious and comically obstinate, backward by preference, clannish and shrewd, are liberal concerning the conduct of foreigners because they are detached. If a Breton household were paid for keeping a herd of gazelles in a corral, they would toss in hay and grain at proper times and in just quantities, and would pay as much attention to the animals' behavior, as long as their charges refrained from making objectionable noises or odors, as the keepers of hotels, taverns and summer lodging places do to their American or English guests. Like all backward, superstitious people who long, long ago devised a means and routine of living in a region which has always been theirs, Bretons who remain in Brittany are curious, not about morals, but unfamiliar little acts, gadgets, buttons and bows, gewgaws, and the ways of foreign men and women with money to spend so recklessly.

I spent my summers as a boy on Cape Ann, where my mother and her people for generations back to Richard Tarr, a founder of the town of Rockport in 1629, "belonged." Therefore I recognized at the small beach of Erqui, where I stayed many weeks longer than I had intended, customs, characteristics, habits and reactions among the Breton fishermen and sailors (and their women ashore) that corresponded with those of men similarly occupied along the New England coast. Those who clung to Celtic dialects behaved almost the same as others who had acquired a kind of French, with that crusty Breton accent that suggests the twang of wires and a provocative or argumentative intent. I went mackerel fishing, as I had done before I was ten years old, with veterans who fished for a living. The ones who had had extraordinary good luck, mostly from inheritances, and who could afford a small crude gasoline motor, were envied by the others, the majority, who still had to row with clumsy oar pins and cumbersome oars. The most advanced Breton fisherman was at least a couple of centuries behind the most backward New Englander. At first, when one mixes with shore and sea folks who, rowing day and night from childhood to the grave, have stuck to a primitive, inefficient pair of wooden pins and oversized, badly shaped, brutally heavy oars, and unbelievably inferior boats, one's feeling is of impatience, even anger. This, as one shares the hours of toil and preparation, shifts gradually to a perverse admiration.

The mackerel fishermen of Brittany, the cod fishermen who sail or ride from Brittany to the Grand Banks, the gatherers of shellfish, squid and octopuses along the Breton rocks, catch mackerel, cod, *langoustines* and *homard*, at a prodigious expenditure of labor, and are obliged to sell them at a pitifully small profit. So many men are lost at sea, or battered to death on the shore, that Breton women wear black practically always for some near relative lost. The number of lighthouses along the Breton shore is as high, relatively, as the losses of life. Bretons never do anything by halves.

If there were a way of determining who are the most stubborn and obstinate people on this earth, all three top contenders would be in France, the land of restraint and reason. My rating would give first place to the Auvergnat, second to the Breton and third to the Basque, but any experienced observer might decide otherwise, that is, the same three in different order. In fact, in every province of France, a faction of the peasantry persists in "the old ways," the more inconvenient the more energetically to be perpetuated. This immovable minority, spread over all corners of France, is reflected and represented in Paris, especially in matters of government, economy and art. It gives the middle class a comfortable satisfaction, and the French middle class, especially the women, exploit provincial servants mercilessly, truly believing such abuse is necessary to preserve the status quo. The frank French employer, male, has not yet got over last century's assumption that an unskilled or organized worker is at heart a public enemy.

We read almost weekly that a certain French "government" has "fallen" and another has been established, by a new Prime Minister and an unstable "majority" in the *Assemblée Nationale*. This

rather comical procedure seldom affects the Frenchman in the street or the Frenchwoman in the home.
Most modern French politicians try to help balance
a mythical budget by chiseling on the gains labor
made in the middle thirties, under what was called
"the Popular Front." Unions and other workers
retaliate. The result is costly, annoying, disrupting,
but the French are used to it, and probably, some
time in the future, will amend their Constitution
and try to improve the "system." So will the English, the Americans and most likely the Armenians,
the Portuguese and the Greeks.

The people of Brittany are less disturbed than
most Frenchmen by governmental upheavals, trivial
or grave. A shocking number of Bretons cannot
read and many others, who can, do not.

The Breton women, who still wear one of the
numerous provincial costumes, are much in demand
as nursemaids and *bonnes à tout faire*. That last
title, maid of all work, means as much as or more
than is implied. The *bonne* who is caught in Paris,
or another French city, from Brittany or any other
province, is not lashed like an ancient galley con-
vict or Roman lady's slave. There would not be
time, and replacements are too scarce. A servant,
man or woman, in a French household, institution,
hostelry, or bar, in the best of situations, does such
a formidable amount of work, over a long period
of hours, for such meager pay, that the average or

worse situations do not bear thinking about. The percentage of growing young Frenchmen who learn about life from a *bonne* is considerable. The number of restless husbands or relatives who are saved by servant girls from getting into real difficulties outside is legion. That the *garçons* do not make themselves equally amenable, and adjust much feminine uneasiness could not be reasonably assumed. The servants in France, drawn from the provinces, contribute mightily to the national unity and international amity.

The prosperous Bretons who become businessmen in Paris generally prosper in lines which have roots in their province. They are hotel men, dealers in sea food, foresters, priests and lawyers. I think the Breton women who marry men from other provinces and settle in Paris, or elsewhere, are stricter and more virtuous than the general run of the female population, being almost invariably pious. Even in fashionable St. Malo, disreputable Brest, or loose St. Nazaire, the women of joy are seldom Bretons, and surely, among the prostitutes in Paris, Breton girls are very rare and inadaptable. Of all the Celts of today, they are the most anachronistic. The Bretons still talk of "independence" from France, when the tax man comes around, and without thinking what would happen to their fish and other commodities if customs barriers shut off their markets. In wars they mobilize as readily and fight as bravely as any other kind of Frenchman.

A large proportion of the lobsters eaten by Parisians and their foreign guests, the tourists, are caught off Brittany, where flourish the *homard* (almost like the Atlantic-type lobster but lacking the meaty front claws) and also the *langouste*, which is like the Pacific shellfish inaccurately called "lobster," although it is delicious when properly prepared. The French know that sea creatures of any kind, the longer they live and prosper in salt or fresh water, the tastier and more tender they are likely to be if adequately cooked. Americans have been conditioned by unscrupulous dealers and stupid self-styled food experts to consume what are called "chicken lobsters," weighing only a pound, and often less. In France, a lobster is man's size. The French do not let themselves be victimized into paying exorbitant prices for slices of certain fish which are shaped like steaks, when other tastier fish, shaped like fish, are available at reasonable fair prices. The French relish the skate, sea urchin, goose barnacle, squid, octopus, eel, sea snail, razor clam, mussel and other natural delicacies wasted by ignorant flavor-blind Anglo-Saxons. An accomplished chef in France creates a masterpiece around the scallop, or St. James shell. In the United States these delectable hinges (scallops) are dipped into some unsavory substance tasting like burlap with sandy crumbs, and fried out of edible existence.

Jules Verne came from the southern edge of Brittany; Chateaubriand from the northeastern corner; Renan, biographer of Christ, was born near the seashore, on the northern coast. Characteristically, the Bretons experienced the Renaissance about one hundred years after the corresponding upsurge was over elsewhere. The most famous military leader, Du Guesclin, was from the wooded area, even today quite distinct from most of Brittany which lies along the coast, all the way from Nantes and St. Nazaire, facing south, around and through Lorient, Quimper, Brest (at Land's End facing west), Lannion (facing north) past St. Brieuc, to St. Malo and Mont St. Michel (an obsession of the late Henry Adams) over the Norman border. Brittany is really in effect a peninsula jutting into the sea toward the west, with as jagged a shoreline as can be found on any map on three of its sides. The edges are rocky, the "mountains" are mere hills, the forests are fantastic, the rivers include all or parts of such important streams as the Loire, the Vilaine, the Rance, the Oust, the Blavet, the Aulne, and twenty-five hundred others no stranger ever heard of, unless by chance.

The fantastic differences between the provincial peoples who, through resistance to Roman domination (and the absorption of many of its benefits), feudal days, Church squabbles, kings both splendid and abominable, the empire, a restoration mostly in name, and four distinct republics, have evolved a unity and deep feeling of nationalism, and loyalty cannot be more strikingly illustrated than by a comparison between the runty, backward, obstinate Bretons, brave and substantial as they are, and the Normans.

Normandy, surely the most vigorous, reliable and powerful province of France, since the eleventh century and especially today, lies along the seacoast and inland to the central Île de France and Picardy, right beside Brittany, the unusual and distorted land with anachronistic Celtic inhabitants. Normandy's great monuments are Mont St. Michel and the Rouen Cathedral, both unique and gigantic. The principal ports are Cherbourg, Le Havre and Dieppe, all three conspicuous in the patterns of modern history and travelers' acquaintanceship and use. The major capital, Rouen, on the Seine, handles the bulk of waterborne traffic and trade between Paris, France and the rest of the world, via Le Havre. The minor capital, Caen, although it was practically effaced in World War II, has charm and traditions, and surviving inhabitants who will restore its ruins and build anew.

In the early tenth century, Normandy was the sturdiest region in what had been Nuestria, and the

Scandinavian Vikings took it over in 911. By 933 the Normans, inspired, invigorated and developed by the most adventurous Northern blood and example, won their independence. A little more than one hundred years later, under their leader, William the Conqueror, they invaded, conquered and left their influence in England, whom no nation has been able to subdue since. The Normans might have conquered and ruled the rest of France, when Normandy was a duchy, had not Duke William died untimely.

Consider the Normans today, still strong in physique and adventurous mentally, the most successful businessmen, the provincials who furnish a tremendous share of artists, scientists, statesmen and soldiers. Their coastline is the best known in the world and their seamen equal the Bretons, but they also have an equal or larger proportion of land men. Their rivers, including the Seine and the Orne, are vitally important. The landscape is the greenest anywhere; the earth is productive; the weather mingles sun and rain ideally for growth. The Normans are industrially minded, also, and make skilled workers, each zealous in his line. In time they converted enough stray soldiers into farmers, who, as peasants, are not stolid or subservient. There is a fellowship among Normans, rich and poor, farmers or bankers, artists or *bons vivants*. In the land of gastronomy, their cuisine tops the rest, with only

Alsace-Lorraine a close second. The regional drink is Calvados, a distilled and aged apple brandy from their own orchards and stills. And Calvados has the Norman qualities. It is strong, non-irritant and smooth. One cannot readily think of any other potent drink which is as good and effective and helpful before a meal, during a meal, and after a meal, also between times.

In Paris the Normans dominate Les Halles, the central markets from which Parisians and visitors are fed. They are always a progressive-conservative, and never a crackpot influence in government. As soldiers they have lost nothing since, in the days of the Vikings, they were the most successful pirates, who brought home the most goods and left behind the least resentment. They are efficient without appearing superficially clever.

The Western world, as, person by person, it eventually visits France and Paris, usually lands in a Norman port and proceeds by boat train or automobile through the Norman fields, along the Seine, between pastures, woods and gardens, and each sensitive tourist wonders how any country can be so lovely, with the most restrained topography. War scars there are now in plenty. They are healing, not festering. One absorbs and recognizes the sky, clouds, light and structure of Poussin and the flair of Géricault; recalls the measures of Flaubert and De Maupassant. Whoever has not tasted tripe *à la mode de Caen*, and duck, underdone as the Rouennais like it, still has a distance to go toward the goal of cosmopolitan progress. Not to be outdone by any cheese geniuses, the Normans invented Camembert.

In New York City, it is a standing joke that no one a transient meets seems to have been born there, although, of course, millions of people actually have been. Parisians are not exclusively native-born. Mostly, it seems, they are provincials from all the quarters of France I have tried to describe, and a few more. In Paris, where the tourist or resident foreigner is likely to spend most of his time, he will be impressed, firstly, by the mutual harmony that prevails among all kinds and types of Frenchmen. The fundamental education of French children is not a local haphazard affair. It is directed and controlled from Paris, with a minimum of ecclesiastical interference or obstruction. Nearly everybody, except Apaches and the moderately or low-priced prostitutes, speaks very good French, and if a slight accent of Marseilles, Strasbourg or Quimper is discernible, the provincial flavor does not distort the language. Even the Parisian thugs and loose women can speak clear, correct French if they are in the mood for elegance or politeness.

Of late years, the Paris police force, the most amiable and humane (to visitors) in the world, has trained a large number of officers, who patrol areas where tourists abound, to speak English. What the stranger must bear in mind is that Frenchmen or women whose English is newly acquired, speak it more freely than they can understand it, when they are on the receiving end and the voice is unfamiliar. What the French officers, clerks, designers, dispensers of luxury goods or staples say to a prospective Anglo-Saxon customer in their kind of English can frequently be assimilated. What the customer says in return may be as ineffective as Chinese.

The Parisians of Norman or Alsatian origin will be the easiest for purposes of communication, and also the smoothest salesmen or women. The Bretons and the Auvergnats will be the most recalcitrant and transparent if they mean to fleece an employer, customer or dealer.

In commenting on the provinces of France, I have selected only those with outstanding and contrasting characteristics, and mostly the ones around the borders of France, and therefore far enough from Paris to be beyond the range of the capital's direct influence, which extends far over the city limits and into Maine, the Ile de France, the Loire valley, and Champagne. The province and capital city of Lyon are too independent and important, as well as too closely connected with Burgundy, for detailed treatment. The Lyonnais, whose mayor has been

Herriot for a lifetime, have everything other people enjoy and fit almost any environment. The group of communities known as the provinces of the Center and the provinces of the West contain much that is noteworthy. In the Center, tourists with transportation visit numerous chateaux, cathedrals and churches, museums and the watering place, Vichy, on which was heaped the worst ignominy, that of being the headquarters of enemy collaborators during World War II. To overbalance that temporary shame, no fault of the real inhabitants, up near Sancerre are the slopes which produce the dry white wine called Pouilly, which many find superior to the wonderful white Burgundy, Chablis.

The Western provinces are relatively bleak, except for a fine long seacoast, including Rochefort, La Rochelle and Marennes, where delicious oysters abound. They sent to Paris such contrasting patriots as Mirabeau and Clemenceau, Mme de Maintenon, and the scientist, Réaumur. They include the Cognac country, Poitiers, Angoulême and the Ile de Ré. Their inhabitants are typical middle Frenchmen, sharing the heritage of the North and the South.

All these various people, from different parts of France, will suffer and die, whenever it becomes necessary, to defend and preserve France as a whole, or the rights, integrity and existence of other provinces threatened from without. The historical, cultural, intellectual and artistic developments have accumulated during more than two thousand years. Just after Columbus discovered America, François I, one of the most cultured monarchs ever to reign anywhere, ruled France. Just before that, Henry VI sat on the throne of England. London goes back to 43 A.D. and therefore is nearly as old as Paris. New York, founded in 1613 by a few Dutchmen, is young. Mutual understanding must take these facts into account, and grant advantages both ways.

8. *The Tourist Trade*

In describing certain of the provinces, I have had no intention of supplying a guidebook. The people of those regions, through more than twenty centuries, have made their differences their common factors, and joined to form a nation which leads the world in culture and the art of living. Whatever Western civilization means or has achieved is exemplified in France; the French have never compromised their essential character to the demands of the machine age. France was not dark in the so-called Dark Ages, nor was it somewhere in the middle in the Middle Ages. It has always been unique. Occasionally, unfortunately, a leader, half-genius and half-insane, has sent France forth on a military adventure that brought him power but warped and corrupted her humane and cultural role in history. Never has she been able to match the barbarity of her neighbors. Having been overrun and despoiled, time after time she has saved herself, either by miracles or by the help of friendly allies.

Mechanically the French seem inept, but the exceptions to this general rule are brilliant indeed. Their scholars and citizens lean more toward pure or theoretical science than the immediately practical. In painting for about three and one-half centuries they have been supreme, as in design (except structural design). French music has never had due recognition, or appreciation, and therefore it contains an immense store of treasures yet to be explored and enjoyed.

The tourist trade, since World War II, has become an important source of sustenance to France, and all other countries reap benefits in proportion. The French Government, in recent years, has done wonders in making it easy for visitors to enjoy the maximum of pleasure, diversion, instruction and self-expansion, with a minimum waste of effort and time. The paintings, for instance, which were ludicrously mingled and scrambled, inadequately catalogued, and illogically grouped and distributed before the last war, have been classified and placed in certain museums, according to period, so that in a few brief afternoons anyone may familiarize himself with the masterpieces of French painting, in the order of the art's evolution and development. The old Italian and Spanish examples remain in the Louvre; the great French school from Poussin to the distinguished group preceding the Impressionists are in the Petit Palais. The Impressionists and their borderline contemporaries have a superb museum of their own in the Tuileries, just off the Place de la Concorde. The Museum of Modern Art, near Passy, on the Avenue de New York (before the war the Avenue de Tokio) has the best samples of the work of post-Impressionists and contemporaries. One need not be an art student in order to form a rational idea of French history, psychology, civilization and progress from a thoughtful consideration of French paintings, reflecting French taste and lucidity covering the entire period the United States has been settled, colonized, stolen from native redskins misnamed Indians, and brought to its present dominant position at the head of the powers of the Western world.

Cathedrals all over France, to which eager women and reluctant males are escorted, are mostly Gothic, therefore antique as to architecture, ancient as to church music and progressive, as far as modern worship is concerned, in advance of any other national division of the Roman Catholic Church. Objective observation of the French, in almost any church at 11 o'clock mass, or vesper services, leads to the conclusion that three-quarters

of the churchgoers are women and that half of the
minority of men would not be there were it not
for the influence of some woman, or women.
Frenchmen who are religious are seldom fanatic,
and those who become missionaries confine their
operations to distant lands. After a disastrous war,
church attendance booms for a while, then dwin-
dles back to normal. Even fifteen years ago, so
many Frenchwomen wore black that a crowd had
a dingy and dismal background. The custom has
lost its hold, to the point that the modern Frenchwoman suffers almost as little from it as an English
or American woman. The signs in dress-shop windows "Mourning clothes in twenty-four hours"
have all but disappeared.

Another healthy evidence that French people of
today are drawing far ahead of Spain, Italy and
South American countries in discarding the draw-
backs of over-Latinization, is reflected in the decline of the undertakers' and funeral directors'
racket which flourished as late as the middle thirties.
In a republic which cherished liberty, equality and
fraternity, a reactionary element of vested interests
had perpetuated the system of first-, second-, and
third-class funerals. I chanced to look into one of
the churches in the town of Colombey-les-deux-
Eglises just after a second-class funeral was over,
and saw the sexton busily snuffing out half the
lighted candles in preparation for a third-class fu-

neral to follow. The two corpses in question had
been neighbors, had worked together, had had
many a drink side by side, belonged to the same
political party (a very conservative one called Radical Socialist), but Monsieur A. had married somewhat above his station as a builder, had prospered
moderately, while Monsieur B. had felt obliged to
make an honest woman of a working girl he had
seduced, and had worked for mere wages. Therefore, when both were called Higher, on the same
day, Monsieur A's affluent widow had to pay a
small fortune for a second-class funeral, with plenty
of candles, while Widow B. got off at one-sixth the
burial expense, in relatively dim surroundings.

If anyone, except me, in the village found the
situation ridiculous or foolish, it was not apparent.

I knew a fine family of Troyes which suffered
real hardship, if not ruin, because a member of the
preceding generation, having strong influence in the
parish, was given a second-class funeral at cut rates
by an undertaker he had helped make solid with
the local Bishop. When a brother of the deceased
who had had an elaborate burial for practically a
song breathed his last, his widow felt obliged to
bury him second-class, and got no price reduction.
She had three daughters who, consequently, were
left without dowries, and all three had to marry
disadvantageously, and lived more or less unhappily
ever afterward.

First-class funerals are for celebrities, and are mostly national affairs, staged without regard to expense. Some time in the late twenties, Marshal Foch expired. I was on the staff, then, of the *New York Herald* and had to help cover the affair. The funeral procession was to begin at nine o'clock, proceeding from Notre Dame de Paris to Les Invalides, via the rue de Rivoli. At five o'clock in the morning someone in high authority noticed that all along the rue de Rivoli, at intervals of about one hundred yards, were "traffic islands" a foot or so above the general street level, where traffic officers and stray pedestrians might find some degree of safety on ordinary days. Such obstructions would play havoc with the million-franc-funeral parade, if the catafalque and whatever followed had to swerve about like ski contestants in a grand slalom. Orders were given, the nearest couple of regiments of the Army were called out of bed, and by 8 A.M., a full hour before the Foch funeral began in Notre Dame, the parade route was clear.

When last I was in Paris, more than twenty years after the incident in question, the rue de Rivoli's traffic safety islands had not been restored, and anyone who tried to cross that famous thoroughfare took his life in his hands.

Of course, French Government railroads, under good republicans or vile traitors, have always had first-, second- and third-class accommodations. The

first class is for the rich and ostentatious; nevertheless it does not guarantee any degree of privacy, except on a few picked trains. Third class is crowded,
dirty, insanitary and uncomfortable; yet the fares,
however low, seem high to poor passengers. Second
class is used by those who feel it is ignoble to ride
on hard boards with unwashed proletarians and
wicked to throw away money for first-class tickets.
Railroad travel in France is an ordeal, always excepting the trains dressed up for international pres-
tige like the Blue Train from Paris to Nice and the
Paris-Rome express, the Paris-Barcelona express, and
formerly the Paris-Berlin express. The French, and
informed foreigners, expect to suffer while riding
on railroads or waiting for trains. The treasury
officials expect all lines and branches will show substantial deficits, although wages are cut below starvation level, and prices are raised as high as any
government dares, at the risk of provoking riots and
revolutions. Having made use intermittently of
French railroad accommodations (far too strong a
word) in the course of thirty years, I seem to
remember that during certain periods they were
worse than usual. The equipment is always out of
date; the tracks and roadbeds are never properly
maintained; the employees, being brutally under-
paid, are likely to be fretful, if not downright
abusive. No one loves the French because of their
railroads, but whoever travels on them can under-

stand readily that France has been impoverished, if not bankrupt since 1914, through little fault of its own. One must take this extenuating circumstance into account, and try to realize what moral stamina and physical endurance are required for a people to transcend such protracted and cruel misfortunes and injustices.

In Chapter Three of this book, I digressed briefly to mention a talented writer, de Montherlant, who is one of the reactionary propagandists known today among liberals as the "last pillars of the Church." Céline, who wrote the magnificent *Journey to the End of the Night*, has been an active anti-Republican, on the Fascist side. Louis Aragon and Paul Eluard, two of the most gifted writers who gave great promise in the 1920's, became Communist ballyhooers, to a degree that is as unintelligent as it is completely ridiculous.

French literature, as may be seen from the few above-mentioned examples, has suffered as cruelly from war and economic chaos as France itself. Simenon, who could have been a Gallic Chekhov, lives and writes in Connecticut. No one can blame him.

André Gide, surely the most profound contemporary French writer, was under suspicion somewhat because of his emphasis on homosexuality, and because he was once bitten by the Communist virus and slowly recovered after visiting Russia.

My point is that during our pestilential century, which turned more than a decade late, many French writers, potentially the most brilliant in our time, have degenerated into extremists, Right or Left, and are of little use as interpreters of France, or true patriots. Others, discouraged, have retired. Writers have less influence today on the French general public than they have in England or the United States. Radio in France is about where it was in America in 1930. Television has not yet become a factor in shaping public opinion or disseminating information. Questions affecting the common good or evil are discussed in cafés.

Since the French contemporary literature which reaches inquiring minds beyond the borders of the country comes largely either from extremists at one another's throats or from a few lingering specimens of the "ivory-tower" persuasion, it is not a reliable gauge of public opinion in France. Foreigners must understand, and it cannot be repeated too often, that each so-called newspaper in Paris is the organ of a small group of special interests, some economic, some political, some anti-social, possibly a few patriotic, according to the editors' and sponsors' lights.

Tourists who go to France from England have not far to travel, but their means are so limited that they are obliged to live in moderately priced hotels and eat in restaurants where they are likely to encounter ordinary French people. The English traveler who is aware of his comedy value, wherever he takes his bit of England with him, usually gets on better with natives, in France or anywhere, than the type who considers his own customs, habits and behavior as universal measuring devices by which the merits of other civilizations must be evaluated.

Tourists from the United States may take as much money with them as they can. Most of them, by European standards, are rich. Of course, the G.I.'s left in France by various wars, and a large number of American students not financed by "the government," live in Paris, months or years, and contribute or acquire as much "understanding" as their capacities permit. I feel sure, after many years of residence in France, that the French are fonder of the Americans who remain incorrigibly American and do not ape their hosts. The simplest Frenchman or woman knows that no outlander is ever going to become French. Frenchwomen who marry foreign men neither lose their native characteristics nor impose them on their husbands. They are wise enough to let well enough alone. If they love an American or a Hungarian, it is because they are drawn toward the unusual. They want the men they love to continue exercising the kind of charm or novelty that won their hearts. Frenchmen will make love to, or enjoy a temporary affair with, any female, from a hopping Hottentot to a pale six-foot Finn, but they seldom marry foreigners. They are quite shy, as a matter of fact, of exotic characters among their own countrywomen when the object is matrimony.

The rich American tourists circulate in a quarter centering around the American Express, the Café de la Paix, the Opera and the Place Vendome, which contains the Ritz, Cartier's, the Morgan bank, Schiaparelli's and, in the shadow of the controversial pillar topped by the figure of Napoleon, any number of taxicabs with disarming and piratical chauffeurs. The flood of Americans who seem to have been put on earth expressly to be confused and fleeced spills over the neighboring Madeleine quarter, the rue St. Honoré, the rue de Rivoli, and the habitable areas near the Place de la Concorde. They frequent the avenue Georges V and all the cross streets between the Champs Élysées and the Seine. Anywhere on the Right Bank, between the rue du Louvre and the Bois de Boulogne, as far as Passy and Neuilly, the American tourists roam.

Formerly the season began in April and ended in September. In recent years, vacationists, avid for fast, painless culture and extravagant bargains in all the luxury trades, are numerous in winter, spring, summer and autumn. The peak is still within the spring and summer months. While American schools are closed during the hot months, the throng is swelled by teachers, mostly female, who, if they are ever destined to stray into the courts of love, shed their inhibitions on shipboard or in Paris. It would be a churlish reader, indeed, who would fail to wish them luck and fleeting happiness.

The region I have described, the Mecca of free spenders, while it is within the city limits of Paris, almost in the geographical center, is served by Frenchmen and women trained to be amiable and clever to the utmost in selling either staples like food, drink, clothes and lodging at deliriously high prices, adjustable to the resources of the client in question, or disposing of luxuries unobtainable elsewhere and quite if not totally unfamiliar to the ordinary Parisian.

A large proportion of the tourists have been in France before, and know their way around the Right Bank reservation. Those can move faster, and spend money with more facility than the newcomers. Most of the women take a quick whirl through the Louvre, a passing look at Notre Dame de Paris through the window of a moving limousine, and a number of the men are guided to the modern equivalent of the old rue Blondel or the House of All Nations. It is a sad but incontestable fact that people accustomed to plentiful but abominable food cannot acquire the taste for high-class fare readily. Neither can plain citizens of an affluent but sketchily civilized land improve their taste easily in any direction or department.

In the face of much discouragement, the French Government provides and subsidizes choice cultural offerings for those who come to France from other lands. I will mention only a few that were available, and very sparsely patronized, the last time I was in Paris. A large section of the Petit Palais was devoted to a display illustrating in amazing detail the almost innumerable stages and advances of animal life on this planet, from the most primitive cells, of an era before the earth's crust was formed, up to the time when homo sapiens had so far outstripped his simian ancestors that his supremacy was well established. There were balconies and walks at various levels around this exhibit, so that anyone could grasp evolution in a few concentrated hours of study and observation more thoroughly than he could learn about it by reading libraries filled with books or listening to thousands of lectures. The most gifted, ingenious and astute scientists of France had collaborated to make this exhibit graphic, clear, accurate and effective. Across the street, in the Grand Palais, throngs were gaping at an annual automobile show that fell far below the standards of more prosperous times. There was always plenty of elbow room around the silent show of evolution, free of charge.

The former prisoners of war held a fair in the Cours la Reine, and in a large temporary gallery set up for the purpose was a definitive collection of Aubusson tapestries, old and contemporary, showing that those patient weavers had caught the modern spirit exemplified in painting by Picasso, Matisse, Gris, Bracque and others. The attendance was negligible.

In a commodious Paris concert hall one evening the municipal orchestra and mixed chorus from Lille performed, in French, a neglected masterpiece of England's best composer, the opera *Dido and Aeneas*, by Purcell. The lights were ablaze, the regimental band of the *Garde Républicaine* in gay dress uniforms animated the lobbies and staircases. For a moment I felt actually sick when I saw the house was nearly empty, knowing how many musicians in my own small range of acquaintance would have given almost anything to attend that performance.

Incidentally, the Northern French performers sang and played as enthusiastically as if they were evoking an adequate response. The French, by the way, are, perhaps, the most sympathetic interpreters of Bach. The best of French music, from the primitives to the moderns, is almost unknown, except by a few scholars and professionals. So much of any culture has to become historical before it is relished as rare entertainment.

Anglo-Saxons are always at least forty years behind time with French painting. A very few years ago London and New York "discovered" Van Gogh (1853-90) and Gauguin (1848-1903).

The plague of large-scale unemployment has seldom, in our era, been acute in France. When commerce and industry, agriculture, the professions and show business cannot take up the slack, larger percentages of the population go to work in some capacity for "the government." There have been times, for instance, and hard times, too, when the French postal service (which includes the telephone and telegraph systems) has been ludicrously overstaffed. But even the thriftiest or most parsimonious Frenchman would prefer to have five men getting in one another's way trying to handle a post-office job any smart adolescent could perform more satisfactorily by himself or herself than to have one family with a breadwinner adequately paid and four others reduced to beggary or crime. As it is, the five families have to get along on near-starvation wages, and have constant legitimate cause for complaint. However, resources, such as they are, are shared.

There is, however, in Paris, a small army of the destitute, shabby, defenseless men and women who have lost their foothold, for whom no place in the current scheme of things can be found. They are allowed to sleep under bridges, along quays, on sidewalks, or to doze in the lowest of cafés until two o'clock in the morning, at which hour they are systematically aroused by the police, and herded toward the central markets, Les Halles. There they may earn a few sous unloading or storing produce from country trucks and wagons, or, lacking that initiative or opportunity, may pick up leaves, fruit or vegetables, any spilled or discarded bits of food, from the busy streets and sidewalks. By six o'clock in the morning, they are back in their hangouts, shelters or lairs, so that those respectable prudent citizens who have eaten their breakfasts with the proper crease in their napkins and start for work or open their shops at a prescribed morning hour are never troubled by the sight of the vagabonds or all-time losers.

The French police and the market folks are quite touchingly kind and familiar in their dealings with the ragtag and bobtail brethren, and when weather permits the latter show a surprising residue of dignity and wit, as if the dregs of life were somehow less abject in Paris than elsewhere. Quite a few die of cold or exposure, of old age or lack of will to continue; not many of actual starvation. It was in Madrid where I met a man reduced to beggary who offered the most direct and fundamental appeal when he asked for alms. I am sure he expressed what the majority of penniless Parisians feel about their appalling situation. The Madrid beggar used to say, after touching his cap deferentially, "Señor. When I was young, the good God took away my desire to work."

True believers were the first to respond.

In Italy and in Spain, begging is one of the important occupations which combine much spirituality with more ingenuity. Latin beggars, in essentially or exclusively Catholic countries, concluded ages ago that they must either disgust and offend the sensibilities of their intended victim, or please and flatter him by means of a superficially agreeable sensation at the moment of approach. In the first instance, the giver shells out hurriedly, to rid himself of noxious sights, odors or reminders. When the beggar is witty or tactful, and as presentable as possible, his clients are inclined to be generous, from admiration of a human comrade who can do so well and make life supportable with such paltry resources.

Nowhere in France is one harassed by beggars. Also the rate of hold-ups, burglary and other forms of larceny (aside from high prices in certain danger zones overrun by tourists) is very low. Private crimes and examples of dishonesty in government,

normally frequent, tend toward the original or sensational. Criminals have to deal with a highly sophisticated, nationally well-organized and progressive *Sûreté Génèrale*, and local police with high
standards of efficiency. Once when I told a French
Commissaire in Paris that in New York no com-
prehensive record was kept of the domiciles of
citizens or transients, criminal or above reproach,
he found it hard to believe that the authorities of
any great nation could be so lax and foolish. He
was equally incredulous when I said that the police
of our large cities did not require the close co-operation of the janitors, superintendents or caretakers
of apartment houses. In Paris, a concierge who fails
to report any suspicious circumstance in his or her
building or neighborhood is in serious trouble if
something goes wrong or someone misbehaves.

If I were asked to designate what I thought was
the principal advantage a Frenchman has over men
of other lands, I should say without hesitation that
his great asset, which enables him to live more abun-
dantly than less civilized males elsewhere, is what
is known as café life. I must hasten to remind the
reader that French café life, an essential part of each
day's existence and pleasure, has no resemblance to
what British or Americans call contemptuously
"Café Society," a rather hysterical phenomenon of

the night. The French had that, too, on Montmartre during the '80's and '90's, up to the outbreak of World War I, centering around the Moulin Rouge, Le Chat Noir, and immortalized in poster and painting form by Toulouse-Lautrec and others.

What I wish to emphasize is the French institution, not for men only but predominantly for men, known as the "apéritif hour." Doctors, lawyers, brokers, thieves, bakers, wage earners, shopkeepers, the great majority of the French male population of any city or town, frequent the cafés of their choice, on out-of-door terraces when the weather is suitable, indoors when the weather is inclement, about half an hour before lunch each noonday through the working week, and for an hour or so before dinner each evening. In Paris it would be hard to find a quarter in which there were not a dozen or more well-appointed cafés, according to local preferences and standards. A sociable Frenchman, therefore, is in contact with at least a dozen of his cronies, enemies, friends, acquaintances, or interesting transients and strangers at least five days each week. In modern France, the "week-end," borrowed from England, changes the pattern on Saturdays and Sundays, and Sunday has always been a day when a French father of a family would probably be at home, or out with his wife and children, dressed in Sunday clothes and usually wishing mildly that the ordeal was over.

The result of discriminating café-sitting is that a Frenchman, without having to arrange difficult appointments, invites Tom, Dick and Harry to dinner the following Thursday, or to go through any of the elaborate routine of making calls, exchanges ideas and renews his relationships each year with thousands of individuals, representing divers interests limited only by his preferences, taste and scope. He hears much directly and overhears even more. He feels the pulse of acquaintanceship, his fellow citizens, his city, department, nation, and of art, science and the Western world. He has his fill of news, convivially interpreted, and of gossip fit for men; he escapes the feeling of being trapped in a domestic vacuum, and still may dine at home habitually, and at regular hours.

There is always one consolation for any foreigner (i.e., non-French individual) who feels he does not understand the French. He may be sure that the French are even more puzzled about him. The millions of sightseers and vacationists who visit France as a rule learn little or nothing about people, excepting a few waiters, chambermaids, guides and fellow-travelers. Resident foreigners in France are fairly numerous, especially in Paris and on the Riviera. Some remain oblivious to the French life around them, and a few others are so deeply impressed with it that they are partly absorbed. The huge majority of men and women now living in countries outside France may grasp the principal problems confronting the French people today, and those who wish may review France's long distinguished history. Everyone must feel live sympathy for the French, bearing in mind that the country and its citizens lack funds because of German (and some Italian) depravity and aggression, and will be in direct line for destruction, atomic, thermo-nuclear or otherwise, and invasion, if Russia and the Communists ever dare to strike, and try for world domination.

Those of us who believe that reason will prevail, and that before Russia and her satellites commit mass suicide or extinguish human civilization, some practical means of continuing what could be an abundant and delightful life will evolve through the efforts of men and women of good will, look toward France. As long as the French can make sweet the uses of adversity, the rest of us should, at least, be able to face the future with the courage of some of *their* convictions.

9. Parisians

Having spent a considerable part of my adult life in France and seen the French through two wars and as many peaces—which truly passed all understanding—I have built up, through the years and vicissitudes, what I like to think is a certain *rapport* with the French. The more clearly one sees those exotic people functioning in their native habitat, the more naturally do they harmonize with their climate, their history, their culture and their social, political, physical, spiritual and everyday needs. Among all the peoples of the world, they are, in their own setting, the least banal and uncomfortable.

When a motion-picture producer or TV director wishes to have personified some creature from another world, or planet, he always ends up with a sub- or superhuman shape in a kind of diver's suit, with an intelligence far superior to that of mortal man, and a kind of relentless malignity. "Destruction on earth and ill will toward man" sums up this Martian or Venusian or Arcturian intruder. Except that he gets nowhere with the beautiful girls of the cast, the intruder represents the frustrated ambitions of the producer or director concerned. He breaks articles without paying for them, frightens and destroys rivals, does not have to dress or buy clothes, and eats blood or carrots without regard to etiquette or flavor.

In the so-called Anglo-Saxon countries—the United States and England, for example—any foreigner who appears as such is viewed as a Martian or Arcturian would be, until he shows an aptitude for selling bananas, playing the oboe, designing hats, singing operatic arias or performing other functions stray foreigners have traditionally accomplished without upsetting Anglo-Saxon ethics or economy. Foreigners among the Anglo-Saxons, before they are refined or plated in the so-called "melting pot," speak dialects of American or English. Otherwise they could talk only to one another. George Bernard Shaw, in speculating on the language or languages spoken in Heaven, decided that the celestial language must be English, since the English-speaking angels would prove incapable of learning foreign languages.

In France, Englishmen and Americans become foreigners, although very few of them suspect it, and most of them would warmly resent the appellation. Up to the last few years, Frenchmen did not travel much. Why should they? The cream of everything was in Paris, and the rest of the world made pilgrimages there, as much to show the French how the others looked and behaved as to soak up French culture or indulge in Babylonian vices. Few of the vices currently practiced in Paris are of French or even Latin origin.

The French, as I have hinted, use ancient and imported vices as tourist attractions, but only the rich French, of whom there are few, can afford to indulge in anything much beyond light wine, vile government tobacco and free dalliance. When I say "free" I do not mean without cost. Everything in France has its fixed price, which can be reduced by tactful bargaining or increased by ostentatious approach. The guidebooks will advise tourists to haggle over prices, no matter how small or how large. Those of us who understand the French would never make such a blunder. We go to any lengths to make the individual Frenchman or Frenchwoman like us, and if we succeed we get the treatment shared by other natives.

Adrienne Monnier's book shop is in the rue de l'Odéon in Paris opposite the building where Sylvia Beach's "Shakespeare Book Shop" flourished for

many years. Mlle Monnier pointed out to me once
that anti-Semitism had never gained ground in
France "because we French also are intelligent, and
therefore not jealous of the Jews." She was referring to the French *intelligentsia*. I think the same
applies to the French businessman, not in the luxury
trades. French businessmen have such a clear sense
of values that they make no attempt to bamboozle
one another. They take the facts of business life for
granted, however harsh and unjust they may appear.
For instance, if one's wife makes off with a penniless actor, somehow absconding with her dowry,
and a businessman's credit is consequently shaken,
his fellow businessmen in France accept his pre-
dicament, squeeze him unmercifully (but without
rancor or malice), and touch wood every time a
man passes wearing the red ribbon of the Legion of
Honor in his lapel.

Lloyd's, which does an immense volume of in-
surance business in France, has accumulated statistics
tending to show that the percentage of cuckolds
among members of the Legion of Honor in France
considerably exceeds that obtaining in ordinary
civilian life. French businessmen in non-luxury lines
are practically all married, and any Frenchman
dreads being a cuckold more than he fears the
guillotine or begging in his old age. There are many
reasons why he should. For Frenchwomen of the
upper middle class, without too much chic or breed-

ing, uncertain of their taste, equipped with servants, and often bored with excessive leisure, develop a frightening tendency to—let us say—"bite the hand that is feeding them." The second-best way they can deflate the ego of their husbands is to carry on a clandestine love affair, which, in France, does not resemble the pristine Dante and Beatrice romance, but, on the contrary, means actual disrobing and cavorting on beds (the lucky ones with American mattresses), the while keeping the secret buried deep in their consciousness (and that of a few hotel workers or servants who regard them and their antics impersonally, unless they want to cut in). A Frenchwoman in that walk of life, enjoying an affair, cannot be made to feel inferior by any husband with an authoritative voice, aggressive manner, and the Midas faculty for trade. All she has to do, to reduce her husband to a pitiful psychological wreck and make him the laughing stock of his business community, is to tell him he has been betrayed.

We were discussing the sense of values. A striking example of French clarity in that department was brought to my attention by a splendid Frenchman of the Haute Marne (in the foothills of the Vosges) who for more than twenty years, including those of World War I and the decade following, was mayor of a delightful little watering place, a town called Bourbon-les-Bains. A battalion of U.S. engineers

was billeted at Bourbon-les-Bains in the summer of
1918. One of the duller doughboys, who became
friendly with the daughter of the widow of a local
grocer, suddenly found himself attending a kind of
solemn meeting on a Sunday afternoon, obligingly
signed a few papers, while being plied with *vin
blanc* (pronounced by members of the A.E.F. "van
blink") and wound up married to the wench.

This mishap of Private Smith started a kind of
epidemic of war marriages between U.S. soldiers
and French females in and around Bourbon-les-
Bains. The adjutant of the American battalion, a
solemn, conscientious, owl-like type, who worked
in a telephone accounting office when not occupied
with the job of making the world safe for democracy, thought it his duty to go to Monsieur Delage,
the mayor, and tell him that the American boys
who were marrying the local women in droves were
not of the better class of American citizens. In fact,
most of them were roughnecks, lowlifes and bums.

I wish the reader could have seen the seraphic
smile on the face of Monsieur Delage when he told
me of his reply to the American lieutenant. Trans-
lated, it went something like this, "Never mind,
Lieutenant. The French brides aren't worth much,
either."

What still puzzled ex-Mayor Delage, however,
years after the armistice, was that the reassurance
he gave Lieutenant Nichols seemed to trouble the

American officer deeply. In America, I explained, the custom is for worthless men to marry the best women, and vice versa. It is a kind of compensation, to keep the population at a truly democratic level. Ex-Mayor Delage is still thinking that one over, since, in France, parents try to marry their offspring to safe-and-sane partners whose status, economic, social and cultural, is not incompatible or incongruous. With the French aristocracy—and there are far too many of them left, one hundred and sixty years after Marie Antoinette, who was not French—it is taken for granted that all men with grand old names are rotters, which is, to all intents and purposes, correct. But some of them are charming.

Count Boni de Castellane, for instance, was one of the first to condescend to an American million-heiress, Anna Gould. Even in the late twenties, when I used to observe Boni de Castellane in the stag line of the Paris Ritz Hotel, tightly corseted and short of breath, he still had wit, and a very soft hand. He had been reduced to cadging his meals, and looking at the ceiling whenever it was his turn to buy a drink, but he was charming, and never were there fewer than a half dozen American society women ready to invite him to tea, and have their names listed with his in the so-called society columns of the Paris *Herald* and/or Paris

Chicago Tribune. The Paris *Daily Mail* had not
then reached the point of recognizing that American society existed at all.

In France, the poor, if they are peasants, marry
according to the advice of their influential neighbors
in the nearest château, or the town priest or doctor,
according to whether they are Catholics or non-
believers. Frenchmen are practically all born Catholics. Those who achieve emancipation, however, do
not become Protestants. They skip that interme-
diary stage, and call themselves atheists, though
they mean agnostics. Or they merely call the whole
thing off. It was James Joyce who, having re-
nounced the Catholic faith, and asked why he did
not join a Protestant sect, replied, "Sir, is it likely
that after having discarded an absurdity that was
logical, I should embrace another that is illogical?"

Joyce was Irish, but in the above explanation he
voiced the feelings of the freer of the French.

While the French sense of values has persisted,
through war and suffering, victory and austerity,
it has been somewhat unhinged by the fluctuations
of the franc, both as to its buying power and its
exchange possibilities in the world money market.
Frenchmen and women who had grown to maturity
before our current series of world wars began, and
now are between fifty-five and ninety years old,
make no attempt to adjust themselves. Each one of

them dates the permanent decline of civilization from some minor or major incident in his or her individual life.

The proprietor of a quiet little hotel in the rue Cassette, Monsieur Valentin Corre, a corpulent, staunch Breton, used to spend nearly all his daylight hours in a dim office on the courtyard, leaning over enormous ledgers and scrawling figures in muddy violet ink with a spluttering, old-fashioned pen. The hotel was in the shape of a U, with two wings and the main building between them. Corre owned one of the wings and the crosspiece, and the owner of the other wing, which was used as a book bindery and rare-book store, offered to sell him the part that would complete the ensemble and give his hotel almost twice its scope and compactness. The price was 150,000 francs, which, in those days, meant approximately $25,000.

In 1949 I stayed at M. Corre's Hotel de Bretagne et du Canada, as I had done, intermittently, since 1923. Valentin Corre had died in the first year of War II. His son, Jean, had been called to the colors, had refused to retreat when traitorous aristocratic French officers of the Pétain-Laval clique ordered the Army to give way, had been taken prisoner by the Nazis, escaped, and had spent nearly five years on the run, working for the underground resistance. Valentin's widow, a trim, plump, sweet-faced, clear-eyed Frenchwoman, as petite and graceful as her husband had been huge and grotesque, had run the hotel during the Nazi occupation; the Hotel Paris-Dinard, commandeered as Nazi secret police H.Q., was a few doors away. One of her devices for retaining her hotel was to recruit old men and pale women with extraordinary coughs and give them rooms at strategic points. Whenever Nazi officers visited the Hotel Bretagne, the alarm was given in time. The cough virtuosi began hawking, spitting, strangling, whooping, gurgling, wheezing and puffing until the old courtyard in front and the verdant little walled garden behind sounded like one of the outer circles of Hell during the rainy season.

Innocent Madame Corre, white hands fumbling her rosary, her shapely body clad tightly in black, would invite the Nazis to make a thorough inspection, at the same time hinting that poor Mme So and So in Room 6 was in a low state from tuberculosis, and that they would have to excuse the appearance of Room 23, since the tenant had suffered a severe hæmorrhage that morning and, what with the shortage of help, she had been unable to clean up. The Monsieur in Room 23, she hinted, had the only kind of hæmophilia which was said to be directly infectious, but what could she do? She could not turn an old client out into the street.

I am digressing from my story. In pre-World-War days, the sum of 150,000 francs had deterred Monsieur Valentin Corre from purchasing the wing of the building which would make his hotel doubly valuable. While I was there, in 1949, I took a short walk over to the rue de Seine, where the small art galleries are. In the window of the Galéries Pierre I saw a large Miro, one of his early works which showed the scope of his perverse imaginative talent, then prophetic of atomic fission, fusion and fuss, as well as fizz, anti-fizz and wham. Most of the canvas was bare, and the few straight or angled strokes of Miro's brush had been so loaded with paint in a loose medium that streaks had escaped, like rain on a window pane. There was the usual suggestion of a germ or a Martian toad taking off for rocket flight, and the All-seeing eye, purely evil, confused with the moon and the sun. I was spellbound and, although I am not a victim of the fatal obsession for owning things I like, I wanted that painting. I wanted it so keenly that it hurt, as if my vitals were being sawn and sutured with raw catgut, looped and tensed inside. I began to calculate the square root of practically nothing, and what to do in France should I go broke and fail to get home.

Knowing Pierre, who, even among art dealers is outstandingly devious, I did not once think of going into the gallery in a straightforward manner and asking the price. By the way, Pierre is a White Russian, and Miro a dainty young Spaniard; at least, he was young when he painted that two meters by ninety centimeters expression of divine frustration of some little thing in the lower foreground who was saying "If germs can fly, why not I," while reaching for a soaring but severed balloon string.

That is the best of the French. So many of them turn out to be Russians, Spaniards or even Visigoths or Siamese. The French do not use a melting pot. Their superiority lies in the sound instinct that such pots usually boil over, leaving the least desirable parts of the broth at the bottom. They coat a foreigner, as if he were a stick of metal in an electrolytic bath of Frenchness, if they wish to Frenchify and claim him. This happens mostly in Paris. In the provinces few foreigners become naturalized. Only after thirty years or so of residence is he accepted and his identification papers allowed to lapse.

It occurred to me that old M. Corre's surviving son, Jean, who was running the old hotel, would be a good emissary to send to Pierre's gallery to ask the price of my Miro. Jean was a war veteran, the father of a family, sent his wife and children to church (at St. Sulpice), and had money in various banks. He had never cheated his clients, and none of them had been able to defraud him to the amount of one sou, which then would not be enough to buy one speck of ground pepper.

What I did not take into account was that Jean's education had been in languages (he spoke German, Italian, Spanish and English fluently, as well as his native French), in the lower phases of the military art, and the French three R's, to say nothing of the hard school of ordinary French business practices. Jean's taste in paintings, alas, was about on the level of Hitler's.

Jean, who liked to accommodate his clients, readily agreed to call at the Galéries Pierre, look at nearly all the paintings with admiration, pretend to disdain the Miro, then casually to ask its price, cash on the nail. The afternoon Jean started on his mission, I set out in another direction on an unrelated errand. I returned just before dinner time and found the Hotel Bretagne, insofar as the courtyard office and the family quarters were concerned, in a lugubrious state. Jean's two small daughters, one nine, the other four, had been spanked and were blaming each other. The young Madame Corre, a very pious, dutiful country girl, was in a corner, telling her beads. The sweet-faced middle-aged Madame Corre, widow of Valentin, was sitting, tight-lipped. She always did that after the younger daughter had been whipped, although she was pleased whenever the older one got it, and not infrequently contributed to the punishment herself.

Jean was nowhere to be seen, and the situation seemed so tense that I did not feel inclined to ask where he was, or how he had fared at the Galéries Pierre. At three o'clock next morning, I heard an unusual sound in the courtyard, which was always closed and locked at night. It was opened by the *garçon,* Albert (pronounced *Al bare*), who slept intermittently on a pallet in the office. Jean Corre was being carried in by a taxi driver and a trusted resistance friend. His young wife was quivering, dry-eyed, in her unbecoming flannel nightgown, and if the two kids were awake they were hiding under beds.

I had known Jean Corre from boyhood and had never seen him drunk. Merry, yes, on holidays, and gala occasions. But this time he was tight, and the bad temper of the early evening which had resulted in family bruises, sobs and consternation had given way to a mood of Silenus plus Fernandel. Somehow, with that unerring instinct of the pickled, he spotted my face behind the shutters of my room. He only railed and yelled that night, with an occasional growl. But gradually, in the next few days, between spasms of double entry bookkeeping and receiving guests, he told me what had happened, mostly to him.

He had not realized, he said, that Americans, especially serious Americans like myself, listed in *Who's Who*, were inveterate practical jokers. He had therefore taken me at my word, had called at the Galéries Pierre, and caught sight of the Miro, with most of the canvas not only bare but somewhat soiled. His reaction had not been mirth but indignation that any reputable dealer (as if there were any) would charge any price whatever for such a monstrosity. The moaning at the bar had aroused the same feelings in honest Jean Corre that a serpent does when it startles a Terrible-Tempered Mr. Bang by squirming under his boot-heel.

Jean had asked the price.

Pierre, knowing his customer was both French and tough, had named a rock-bottom price: 150,-000 francs.

When Jean Corre had realized that some fool American was going to pay the same number of francs that had scared his good father from completing their hotel deal, Jean went berserk. He groped his way from the gallery to the nearest bar and threw in a few quick *marcs de Bourgogne*. He then drove home blindly, endangering his own and several strangers' lives, belabored his girl children, upbraided his horror-struck young wife for having donated fifty francs to some charity a nun was collecting for that day, called his bottle companion from the underground, disappeared into the cellars of the St. Germain des Prés region where night life now centers, and got himself so drunk that he could not walk, but was able to laugh again.

In 1949, the price of that Miro—150,000 francs—was approximately $5,000. This was far beyond my means, so I am still without it, and would be inclined to fix the Scribes' Curse on any reader who takes advantage of this confidence and toddles over to the rue de Seine to buy it.

So do not imagine, dear reader, that "the French" are so decadent that they go crazy over the abstractions of Matisse or the gremlins of Gromaire. They think of art in terms of Rosa Bonheur, as Americans identify it with Maxfield Parrish, and the English with Gainsborough's "Blue Boy."

I encountered an especially piquant example of middle-class French taste while editing a semicultural page for the Sunday edition of the *New York Herald* in Paris. In order to have a few features that would not cost Mrs. Ogden Reid any of the vast sums of money she seemed to be planning to take with her, after death, I contributed a weekly article on the "modern" French painters, beginning with Poussin, who died in 1655. I had worked my way through Claude Lorrain, Watteau, Fragonard, Chardin, David, the fine old rake Boucher (who died while painting a Venus from a nude model), Daumier, Corot, Courbet, Delacroix, the Impressionists all the way from Pissarro to Monet, Manet, Toulouse-Lautrec, Cézanne, the Dufys, Bracque, Rouault, etc., and when I got to Matisse realized I was running out of French painters. But there was still Picasso, the Spaniard who had adopted France and the whole modern world.

Picasso's studio was not far, in those days, from the *Herald* office in the rue de Berri. I had met him through Gertrude Stein, so I called, explained my series of articles, and he gave me willingly a pen-

and-ink drawing, of his period of "classical" heads, to be reproduced in my article.

I used to make up the Sunday page on Saturday evening, as early as I could. When the block of the Picasso head came down I dashed off a hand proof and saw, to my horror, that the Frenchman in our alleged "art" department had decided that Picasso's drawing was false, so the chap had retouched and "corrected" it. There was barely time to have the drawing restored and another cut made. But I kept a proof of the "corrected" drawing for Picasso, who treasures it to this day.

Wherever one goes, there is a bevy of stuffy French professors who believe that their mission on earth is to ferret out errors in other folk's creative or interpretative work. Each time one of my articles appeared, I received letters from some of those condors. In the case of Watteau, where there was a question as to whether or not he dallied with his sister-in-law because he had one of history's prize misfits for a wife, I ventured to express the hope that the suffering painter had consummated the affair, and enjoyed it. The number of obscure, irate and expendable Frenchmen who resented my suggestion that Watteau had sinned astonished me. The French are not given to excesses of zeal, and one finds no equivalent of our Puritans among them, except in academic circles where old men, if they are not protesting about something, can scarcely be said to be existing at all.

French art experts, although they are livelier than English and American semi-journalists who have views about paintings, are far from being infallible. About the time some of their senior members were abusing me regarding Watteau, it came out that the Louvre had bought, and paid high prices for, two false Watteaus which were then on exhibition in those sacrosanct halls. All Paris laughed at the experts' expense. The cafés were enlivened with comment at the *apéritif* hour. In America, if a news item to the effect that a couple of fake Rembrandts had got into the Metropolitan Museum were reported in the *Times*, no drinkers would care. Of course, in fairness it should be pointed out that any museum in England or the United States which did *not* have a couple of sham Rembrandts would provide a truly sensational news story. In the same way prestidigitators use black backdrops to render black threads invisible to the audience, purveyors of questionable old masters use the dim light of Holland, the only light Rembrandt had, in which to carry on their devious functions.

The French general public, while it cares as little for art as do publics elsewhere, reacts with glee to any kind of fraud, and always sides with the crook, even when taxes are high and public monies find their way into disreputable channels. The French do not gather in large numbers to watch an ordinary guillotining, however, because the loss of man power, even criminal man power, depresses them. This is one of the essential characteristics of the French. This deep-rooted regard for man power prompted the French legislators and authorities years ago to forbid the drinking of absinthe, made of *artimnesia santonica*, on the mistaken theory that the absinthe habit is detrimental to the birth rate. French doctors testified that an absinthe appetizer leaves a man and/or a woman feeling so content with things as they are that he or she is loth to exert himself or herself.

As in so many cases, when the French or any other Solons wish to correct an evil, the cure proves worse than the disease. Nothing in the way of prohibitive legislation ever backfired worse than the anti-absinthe statute. The liquor manufacturers devised a substitute called Pernod, made from *anis* and other loose herbal ingredients. Pernod, as a matter of fact, makes a drinker quite crazy, if he indulges in it a little too much. Remember how Raimu behaved that afternoon in *The Baker's Wife*. His outburst was the result of a bottle of neat Pernod.

I am sure Ralph Franz, the present art editor of the New York *Herald Tribune*, will not resent my recalling our Paris days and what happened to him after seven Pernods, properly diluted with cool water. We were both connected for a while with the *Chicago Tribune*, Paris edition. I had left about six weeks before the evening in question in order to devote more time to *transition*. However, that night I went to dinner in the little *Tribune bistrot* run by a Monsieur and Madame Gillotte. The dining room at the rear seated eighteen, and seventeen were present when Franz came in, looking somewhat glassy-eyed. He took the one unoccupied chair, placed it carefully under the single light bulb in the center of the ceiling, and began to take off his clothes, draping each garment over the chair. He thought he was in his hotel room, at least three miles distant.

We put him to sleep on a bench in the Gillotte kitchen, and I took his place on the night city desk. By the time he awoke, wishing he had never been born, the Paris *Tribune* was ready for the presses, or as nearly ready as it ever was. Unluckily I had had a few, myself, not Pernods but shots of Calvados, with the result that all the top headlines across the front page covered datelines from Washington, D.C. None of the subscribers complained. The only way we could be sure we had any readers for that sheet was to make an error in the baseball results, or in the quotations on the New York Stock Exchange. A slip in either of those departments brought showers of protests, in person, by phone, by letter, or telegram.

I think the reason so many French or Francophile artists use absinthe addicts as models is because Pernod drinkers will sit still for hours on end, looking as dejected as a candidate just enrolled in hell while thinking who knows what beautiful thoughts, some doubtless of an amatory nature.

The anti-absinthe statute reminds me of a city ordinance of Paris which forbade any registered prostitute to stand under a street light. At one time, before the accursed post-War II reformers got started, the only two acts forbidden in Paris that I could readily call to mind were drinking absinthe and, applicable only to a section of the female population who deserved better, the prohibition against standing under lampposts. There was another "don't" law, come to think of it. Bastards could not be given a saint's name at their christening, and a French official had a dim office in one of the government buildings, where he composed unsaintly monikers for the dear love kiddies. Most of them he put together from syllables occurring in Greek or classical mythology. Others he took out of Molière.

Somewhere back in this text I wrote that Frenchmen, those who came before the last modern crop, seldom, if ever, traveled. French married women, before De Gaulle emancipated all Frenchwomen with a stroke of his pen, could not travel on trains or steamboats without written permission from their husbands. In one extreme instance, about 1928, a woman of my acquaintance, French from top to toe, and the wife of a French army officer then on duty in Algeria, got word that her husband was dying of the flux. Her impulse was to hurry to the deathbed and give the captain what comfort she could. Paris officials and railroad officials, who interpreted regulations strictly, would not let Madame go to Algeria. Her husband was too weak to sign the required permission.

A Frenchman's home is indeed his castle. It is seldom one is invited there, except for some ulterior purpose. If a Frenchman should arrive home, unannounced, and find a man calling on his wife, even if the man were the Frenchman's closest friend, there would be violence and sword- or gunplay, unless husband and wife had agreed to let each other go their own way. Even if such an arrangement obtained, the wife would be expected to meet her men friends, discreetly and secretly. Most husbands, however, like to have priests in their homes, unless it is too late at night. And the French clergy, certainly the most cultivated, sophisticated, urbane and companionable priests in the world, would be most unlikely to take unfair advantage of the hospitality of their own parishioners. Should a French priest be as clumsy as that, he would be sternly reproved by his Bishop. French priests are not fanatical about celibacy, but they like to have their own parishes without blemishes traceable to them.

I was told that a man of the St. Severin parish, who had been arrested for misbehaving with a girl below the age of consent, when reproached by his priest in the course of a confession, retorted irritably: "Do you mean to tell me, Father, that you have never had a girl under age?"

"Evidently, I may have. But the police knew nothing of it," the priest replied sternly.

France is proud of her clergy, and should be. In any other land we could mention, the Church is chiefly concerned with this education of seminarians and members of the priestly orders. Scholarship with the French clergy reaches heights not overtopped in the secular world. Only three or four years ago, for example, the Order of Carmelite Brothers undertook a study of Satan, his status, his history, his significance. They published their findings, with essays by the foremost critics, theologians, anthropologists, psychologists and other specialists, including Emile Brouette, Père Bruno de Jesus-Marie, Dr. Françoise Dolto, and P. Joseph Henninger, S.V.D. of the Anthropological Institute.

Americans owe a considerable debt to Father Henninger, in particular, for his tireless research in the field of the religions and beliefs of North

American Redskins. He writes succinctly and eloquently of the "Indian" devil called Coyote. The Indians of Northern California, who reached a very high cultural level, believed that Coyote introduced death into the world, in order that elaborate funeral ceremonies might be organized. Our Indian Devil was a pushover for any kind of feast or celebration, it seems. When good fellows got together, with or without squaws, Coyote got in his niftiest work, and he thought it worth-while to introduce as radical a phenomenon as death in order that there should be music, baked meats and social gatherings.

The Delawares, according to Father Henninger, accused their Satan, one Nanaboush, of having invented work. The Supreme Creator, they believed, was so busy during the brief period of creation that he did not notice, as he fashioned the sky, sun, moon, stars, then men and animals, that a questionable character He had not created Himself was manufacturing flies, mosquitoes, monsters and men, women and beasts without good will. When the Great Spirit began making it tough for Nanaboush's protégés, Nanaboush fought back. Hence the struggle between Good and Evil which continues today, and will rage forever.

Almost any Frenchman, excepting the tight-faced bourgeois kind who identify themselves with the Deity in playing the grave and responsible husband and running a profitable business in staples, feels that any strange or exotic influences are likely to affect him, personally, sooner or later. Hence the thrill they enjoy when reading or hearing about Redskins, the Devil and his cohorts, and, in the old days, Americans (North) who were all treated like eccentric millionaires with arrested development.

In the early days, while North America was being settled, if that is not too strong a word, the French priests and explorers learned about the Red Men, and were fascinated and uplifted. That the missionaries went through the motions of converting Indians to Catholicism was not taken too seriously by either party. By and large the Indians were willing to oblige, and to submit to baptism. In return, the visiting French priests did not complain too much if the Indian retained his old beliefs, along with the new one, provided he was willing to relate old tribal legends for translation into French. Thus some fairly picturesque tales got into circulation throughout France concerning the Redskins, and persist to this day.

I took some French lessons from the late Abbé Alphonse Lugan, a Jesuit missionary attached more or less to St. Sulpice. Monsieur l'Abbé was a rugged, forceful type, who had written superficial books in French and English about American politics. He gave me a French reader which contained the following story, and furthermore, this fine specimen of French health and culture, who had seen at first hand most parts of our world, did not find the tale implausible. Naturally, I, admiring the priest's naïveté in a character for whom humility was vitally important, did nothing to spoil it.

The protagonist of the story, one Jean-Baptiste Mercier, joined a French exploring party in the middle seventeenth century, was lost in the wilderness somewhere along the Delaware basin, and was captured by the dread Lenni-Lenapes. His first evening in captivity was spent in the center of a circle of tribal counselors, which included the chief, Magabagadoosh. Although Jean-Baptiste understood nothing of the Lenape language, he soon realized that the tribesmen were discussing his head, which was prematurely and completely bald.

One of the chief's tepees was situated near the glowing campfire. Jean-Baptiste had been placed as close to the fire as was consistent with comfort, so the play of the flames was reflected in the prisoner's dome. The chief's daughter, Winking Muskrat, peeping through a slit in the tepee door, saw this amazing white man whose head shone like a polished agate, and wept because she knew he was slated to be scalped.

Finally, the chief made a gesture to one of the more impressive braves, magnificent in war paint. The brave drew his long knife, and tried to get a skin hold on Jean-Baptiste's scalp. It proved impossible. There was a gasp of surprise when Winking

Muskrat, disregarding the taboo that females must not interrupt males in executive session, came forth with an ornamental phial which she offered to the chief, at the same time making an impassioned plea for a stay of Jean-Baptiste's execution. The chief grunted, and consulted the elders. And the elders, knowing how it pained their leader to deny anything to his darling daughter, accepted her suggestion, to wit: Winking Muskrat and her mother had learned of a secret formula for growing and preserving luxuriant hair. The mixture was in the phial. So each day, from then on, Jean-Baptiste was visited by a junior medicine man who rubbed the ointment on his scalp. Not a week passed before Jean-Baptiste, with mixed feelings of joy and regret, felt a fine fuzz sprouting all over his head.

A few nights later, he was visited by Winking Muskrat, who, mad with love and determination to save her white man, had slipped knockout drops in the waterskin used by the guards and was offering her all. Jean-Baptiste, for the honor of France, did his virile best, so that she emerged dizzier than ever, more rapt and abandoned, and was ready to forsake her own people for a life in France.

"In France, one has to have money," Jean-Baptiste said, sighing. Obviously Winking Muskrat and he could not cart away enough wampum for a day at Longchamps races, let alone a life of delirious love. But he was practical, and she was co-

operative. She knew the formula for the preparation that would grow hair, and was prettily sur-
prised when Jean-Baptiste made her understand that
France was so far behind the Lenapes in development that French chemists and charlatans had been
trying in vain, during many centuries, to find or
make a concoction that would grow hair on bald
heads.

They planned their escape and set out on a moonlit night only twenty-four hours before Jean's scalp,
now thick with dark wavy hair, was scheduled to
be lifted and preserved as a tribal relic. The Lenape
braves pursued the eloping couple, and to save Jean,
his noble mistress gave herself up, to delay the detail. Jean finally reached what is loosely called
"civilization," brought the formula to France, and
became independently rich. In some way, however,
he had got the prescription wrong, and the stuff he
made would not grow hair, but with his own head
to exhibit, and a line of sales talk he had picked up
in Manhattan on his way home he sold several hundred thousand shares in the company, and if his
product did not work any better than the oint-
ments, salves and lotions of his competitors, his
Lenakerine Hair Tonic was no worse, and, in fact,
proved cooling, cleansing and otherwise harmless.

Before Jean was married, to the daughter of a
family which would have spurned him before he
got rich, he confessed to his fiancée that his heart

had been lost in the Delaware wilderness and that, on moonlit nights, he still shed a tear on his pillow for Winking Muskrat, who let herself be tomahawked that he might live.

After that, and the wedding, Madame Jean-Baptiste Mercier was desperately jealous of all young women with long black hair and a reddish complexion. Otherwise things went smoothly for the Merciers. The moral: Never tell your wife about the past.

French families are closely bound together and the destinies of the members constitute a pattern or a tangled skein. The Gillottes, who ran the famous little *bistrot* behind the *Petit Journal* building in which the *Chicago Tribune* (Paris edition) was edited, composed and printed, are typical of a large and vital section of the French population, who own small cafés and restaurants, and through years and generations acquire bigger and better places, or else die of overwork. The French term for willingness to work is "courage." Let that sink in.

Few Frenchmen had more "courage" than Monsieur Gillotte, although he was somewhat undersized, had a head as bald as that of the legendary Jean-Baptiste Mercier, and wore a perpetually amiable grin which would better have suited a mental defective. Madame Gillotte, plump but hard as nails, and no taller than her agreeable husband, was the dynamic one. She worked twice as hard as anyone else in her bistro, and drove each one of them to the limit.

The quarter in which the Gillotte bistro flourished was an interesting one which showed signs of life night and day. The *Métro* station Cadet was at the intersection of the rue Cadet, the rue Lafayette and the rue Rochechouart. Across on the northeast corner stood the huge *Petit Journal* building which was one of the most complicated, architecturally, I ever got lost in. Those of us who worked on the *Tribune* were likely to get bewildered in the labyrinths constituting each floor and once every three times at least had to shout for help and guidance to find the offices we used, however irreverently, each night or day.

At a sharp angle, the rue Lamartine, which skirted the *Petit Journal* building at the rear, entered and crossed the rue Rochechouart, two doors from a first-class lupanar which closed at two o'clock, according to city regulations in that *arrondissement* (the 9th, close to the border of the 10th). But for the night workers and late wayfarer, Madame Marcelle opened up again, via a side door, at 2:05 A.M. The *Chope Cadet*, nearest the *Metro* station, was open all night, too, and furnished a warm blaze of light. The *Rendezvous des Scribes*, on the corner of the rue Lamartine and the rue Rochechouart also kept going twenty-three hours daily. By a neighborly arrangement, the *Chope Cadet* closed between five and six every morning, in order that it might be cleaned and freshened up. The *Rendezvous* did likewise between six and seven. So the clients of either café had only to walk fifty yards for shelter during the necessary cleaning hour.

There was another large café, with the most elaborate restaurant, moderately high in price, called the *Restaurant Lamartine*, across the narrow rue Rochechouart from the *Rendezvous des Scribes*. I have enumerated and described these three huge continuous drinking and eating places to give an idea of the competition the brave Gillottes endured and transcended. Come to think of it, there was another place, a wine shop run by Italians and specializing in Asti, either still or "spumante," which is one of the trickiest semisweet wines ever fermented. Much that is unstraightforward in the Italian character must be due to the popularity of Asti wines. One bottle in twenty will put one to sleep as if one had been malleted and drugged. The next will start one on a hectic period of three-day wakefulness that often ends in unemployment or in quod. To drink Asti in any appreciable quantity amounts to an invitation to the criminal population to roll one. The French do not drink Asti unless they want to commit a crime of violence which, under the soothing influence of Bordeaux or Burgundy wines, would never come off. And how bitterly the French complain, about Italians in general and all things Italian, if chance deals them one of those sleep-laden bottles of Asti and instead of breaking a brother-in-law's nose they fall asleep in an alley and are robbed of cash, shoes and trousers and shoved into an ash can, without remembering enough to identify their assailants or prefer charges.

All the foregoing comes under the heading of competition for Madame Gillotte, whose place was only fifteen feet wide, and fifty feet deep. On the street frontage was the bar, and below, the wine cellar eight feet by twelve, which also served as family sleeping quarters. The small dining room in which Ralph Franz tried to undress was behind the barroom, and farther back was the kitchen, small but somehow adequate.

Monsieur and Madame Gillotte bought the place —the ground floor and the basement or wine cellar—with their savings and her dowry, just after they were married. Their only son was begotten in that cellar, where dust clung to old bottles and the fragrance of wine and cheeses prevailed over no matter what. The son was nicknamed Bobo, and for him they acquired a few years later, the largest, goofiest and blackest dog in the quarter, called Toto. I think Toto was out of a Great Dane by a Doberman. Toto had a tail that was almost hairless and as long and strong as a bullwhip. This he swung continuously, grinning foolishly the while, and in a place the size of the Gillottes' a tail of those dimensions could not be wagged without colliding with something or someone.

The only thing Madame Gillotte loved more than work and the slow accumulation of money for a "rainy day" was her son, Bobo, and those of us who admired Madame Gillotte often wondered why—even after we had made due allowances for the maternal instinct. It was a tossup, in fact, as to which creature was the more useless and less promising, Bobo or Toto. Me, I voted for Bobo, as the absolute low in utility and intelligence. Bobo was not an idiot. He was a sap. He grew fatter and lazier, in the midst of such parental examples of industry and thrift as would have inspired Peck's Bad Boy to pitch in and help them. In school Bobo was advanced from time to time, merely because the Gillottes contributed regularly to the nuns.

When, in late 1925, I became a proofreader on the *Chicago Tribune* (struggling with copy which had been written by either drunken or illiterate American exiles and set up by French compositors who confused English with Canadian French), Bobo was approaching what in a normal specimen would be called "puberty."

Throughout those years of honest toil, Madame and Monsieur Gillotte, having achieved Bobo, gave up what the priests like to dismiss as "family duty" and slept in relays. Madame knew that a bistro, with its doors closed and locked to customers, makes no profits. So the Gillotte place, like the important *Chope Cadet,* the Lamartine and the Scribes' Rendezvous, was open for business day and night, with Sundays, Mondays and holidays, Easter and Christmas thrown in. Bobo, who was better at sleeping than anything else, dozed beside whichever of his parents was off shift. Monsieur Gillotte, entrusted with the bartending, cooking and serving from 2 A.M. unto 6 A.M. and in the dull hours of the afternoon, from three until five, carried on while Madame got her six hours' rest. Monsieur, who required a full eight hours, slept from 10 P.M. until 2 A.M. and from 6 A.M. until 10 A.M.

Madame, the real boss, therefore, worked eighteen hours a day, or 126 hours a week. That is not unusual for French citizens who have small cafés or shops or who sell their services or products as artisans, for themselves. Even today, with all the labor agitation, the unions, an ever-growing social consciousness throughout the lower classes, and the power of the women with the vote, a man who has to work for wages for an employer who shares no family or group interests with him is considered by the rest of French society as being only one degree above the level of the tramp or vagabond. Unorganized workers are used and disposed of as if they were robots or beggars. They are, in some ways, held in more distrust than beggars, who, if only because of their sympathetic mention in the New Testament, are granted by most Frenchmen to have souls. In the mind of the middle-class French businessman—even as likable (in other respects) as my good friend, Monsieur Pharamond, who runs the finest market restaurant in Paris, or Jean Corre, of the Hotel Bretagne—organized workers are public enemies, to be dealt with by the police, armed with loaded canes, long billies, ready boots and oiled automatics or machine guns.

The luckiest men in France have money through inheritance and a business or profession which enables them to live without dipping into capital. Then come the smart men who, without a big stake to begin with, are able, by thrift and application, to amass a fortune for their children, and thus lift them into Class One. The next group, who cannot achieve a business or profession of their own, seek to attach themselves to some family connection who controls a going concern. These learn the taste of boot polish at a very early age. Then come the tinkers, scissors grinders, street peddlers, mountebanks, concierges, glass setters, window washers and chimney sweeps.

Lastly, those who work for wages for a stranger or a soulless company. One hears too much about the Communist Party of France, which at its height, just after the occupation, had one-third of the votes in the *Assemblée Nationale*. Now only about one-

fifth of the people's chosen representatives are ac-
knowledged Communists, and most of them come
from two powerful unions. Not many union industrial workers have what could be described as
"homes."

Red propaganda and influence have not pene-
trated the French middle class, generally. Small independent business people, like our Gillottes, while
they seldom have time to attend church, either
curse or cross themselves at the mere mention of
Marx, Lenin, Stalin or Soviet Russia. That does not
mean that the middle-class Frenchman wants to
suppress Red newspapers, or forbid Reds the right
of assembly, or even the privilege of shooting off
their mouths. The French respect civil liberties,
except under extreme provocation. The way to
deal with subversives, the French think, is never to
buy from them (unless the bargain is truly tempt-
ing) and under no circumstances to hire them or
give them shelter.

Monsieur Gillotte, who worked only sixteen
hours a day, or 112 hours a week, and not at the
pace set by Madame, which would have killed him,
did not complain. He had the same objectives as his
wife, and was almost as fond and indulgent as she
toward the scion of the bistro, Bobo.

The cellar was damp but the Gillottes were of
hardy stock. Their stamina kept them from being
seriously ill, but the chill and dampness of their

sleeping basement prevented them from ever being
entirely free of colds. Bobo never caught cold because, I am sure, he would have been too lazy to
cough.

Madame Gillotte's dream was to give Bobo the
educational advantages she herself had not had. She
was determined he should graduate from the Sorbonne, and have a legacy of 1,000,000 francs with
which to buy a place as important as the *Chope
Cadet*, near an active *Métro* station. Monsieur Gillotte asked only of life that he get by each day and
hour without irritating Madame and being what the
French call *attrapé*—nagged.

It is a tribute to the elasticity and humanity of
the Catholic schools in France, which are tolerated
with a shrug of indifference and helplessness by
most patriots and scholars, that Bobo finally got
into the equivalent of a *lycée*, or junior college.
Bobo had never been whipped, except accidentally
by Toto, with that deadly tail. In my case that tail
was responsible for a subsequent case of house-
maid's knee I developed years later. Toto cracked
my left kneecap while I was busy with a *cassoulet
toulousain* cooked by Madame Gillotte, and a liter
of a Bordeaux white wine known in the Cadet
neighborhood to this day as "Bordeaux Paul." I was
that much attached to it, and the local patrons did
me that honor, of naming the wine, unofficially,
after me. It is grown and made on one of the lesser

slopes near Monbazillac and while it was available, never did I feel the need for barbiturates or Benzedrine products. I can close my eyes here at my typewriter and enjoy its bouquet, and feel its smooth coolness down my throat, and taste it with the side of my tongue.

The work at the Gillotte *bistrot*, what with the expansion of the *Tribune* and *Petit Journal*, proved too much even for Madame Gillotte and Monsieur. Madame suffered actual pain at the thought of paying any help from the profits, and thus delaying the day when Bobo should have his college diploma and a million francs, or its equivalent at the rate of exchange that might then prevail.

Just then one of Monsieur Gillotte's poor relations, a red-headed virgin of forty, dropped in, hoping for a free meal and some coffee. Her name was Philomène and she wound up by being hired. Philomène had a well-rounded bust and good legs, her hair was light and fluffy, and her eyes were slate blue. It had not been moral scruples which had kept her intact. She had been determined not to part with her principal asset without getting something substantial in return, a *quid pro quo*. That could only mean, in her direct way of thinking, a man who would support her for life.

Naturally every member of the neighborhood newspaper staffs, French or American, made passes at Philomène, but she tolerated them without showing too much displeasure. Madame Gillotte suspected her, but was too busy to watch her constantly. The two women, superficially polite and pleasant with each other, worked up a vibrant hatred. Nevertheless, because Philomène was a relative of Monsieur Gillotte's and worked for low wages, with an idea in the back of her head that she would do well for herself, somehow, with so many eager men around, she did not quit and was not fired. She played up to Monsieur Gillotte, who, knowing his wife's animosity toward the redhead, scarcely dared look at her.

The first offensive move by Philomène, in the match with Madame Gillotte, was to taunt the latter indirectly about sleeping with her son, who had just turned sixteen. Somehow, while waiting on some women in the back room, Philomène directed the conversation to the subject of relationships between mothers and sons. These paying customers went so far, having been tipped off, as to reproach Madame Gillotte for her immodest minor economy. Madame Gillotte turned so white I thought she was going to strangle the women, but she controlled herself and sent for the priest. He said Bobo should have a room of his own; so Bobo left the parental bed in the wine cellar, and slept next door, in what had been a servant's tiny cubicle in the attic above the Restaurant Lamartine.

Next, Toto disappeared. The police, the customers, God in heaven, and He knows who else, were invoked, but no trace of the dog was ever found. I had noticed, however, that Philomène frequently had kicked the poor beast when she thought no one was looking. Also that she kept an old-fashioned hat pin in her fluffy red coiffure in order to stab Toto when his feeble yelp would be covered by the rumble and rattle of a passing *camion*. Certain it is that Philomène, in the days following Toto's disappearance, went about her duties gaily and indulged in humming tunes, the words of which were ofttimes *risqué*. Madame Gillotte, for once, did not suspect Philomène. The dynamic *patronne* simply could not conceive that a human being would abuse or deprive an inedible pet of life. I, for one, began to look more closely at this devious unfulfilled redhead, a maid at forty, who could contrive to dispose of a body the length and size of Toto's, with or without the butcher's tools or art, in a compact little *bistrot* each inch of which was utilized and in a quarter as active, twenty-four hours each and every day, as our precious little triangle around the *Métro* Cadet. The total disappearance of Toto was a mystery beyond the powers of solution of the newspapermen, all amateur sleuths, who held forth so brilliantly on criminology at the Gillotte bistro.

It was understandable that Philomène should prefer working during the hours Monsieur Gillotte was about and Madame was asleep. It was also necessary, since, with the best will in the world, Monsieur could not handle brisk trade with the efficacy of Madame Gillotte. Anyway, Philomène, who loved the night, stayed on duty from 11 P.M. to 9 A.M., besides helping with the dinner between six and eight, at which last-named hour the newspaper crews started the night shift. That left Philomène from 9 A.M. until nearly 6 P.M. in which to sleep and primp. The only room available for Philomène in the immediate neighborhood (aside from about two hundred the *Tribune* and *Petit Journal* men were anxious to place at her disposal) was in the building next door to Bobo's sleeping quarters.

A few months after Philomène became employed by the Gillottes, a charming young tenor named Bernardi, whose father was Italian and his mother Australian, blew in from Sydney and needed a job to bolster his cash supply and enable him to continue his studies, with a view to singing at the *Opéra Comique* as a proper springboard for an operatic career. Bernardi was tall, but not too tall, with an agreeable Australian accent, robust health and a merry brown eye. We all wished him the best of luck, and were more than willing to give him the benefit of our counsel. We took him on as proofreader, of which the *Tribune* rated four, and the other three gladly supervised and shared his work until he learned the marks, signs and proof routine. Bernardi being bright, that took less than a fortnight.

About 2 A.M. we all put the *Tribune* to bed and, to ease our consciences, forgot every word that was in it. Somehow we always made our deadline and the *Tribune* caught the early trains, bound for everywhere in Europe. Bernardi and I frequently sat next to each other when the bunch hustled into Gillotte's in the early hours for a snack and six or eight nightcaps. If we were on the dot, we would see Monsieur Gillotte coming up the ladder from the wine cellar, unwashed but alert. Madame would offer her face to be kissed on one cheek, then the other. Then she would descend the ladder to the family bed, which would be warm. Madame on retiring and Monsieur on awakening would be reminded, by a certain emptiness in the rumpled bed that Bobo, the heir and beneficiary of their years of self-denial, was in another building, and each would feel a twinge. Bobo, just then, one hundred to one, was feeling nothing at all. He never tried to do his homework after his first and only attempt which had resulted in a headache.

As soon as Madame was safely down the ladder, Philomène would drift out of the kitchen, freshly aproned, her fluffy hair in order, and redolent of Quelques Fleurs. She would, in greeting her "uncle," sidle up to Monsieur like a skiff to a landing when the breeze is inshore. As faithful and true as Monsieur Gillotte was to Madame perforce, he would nervously glance over his shoulder toward that cellar trap door before smiling at Philomène, letting his eyes stray down to her bosom, and wishing her good day.

By some odd chemistry none of us can hope to understand, the first night Bernardi came with us into Gillotte's, and brushed by the freshly combed and perfumed waitress with the hair between Titian and Renoir, with possibly a dash of Gainsborough or Puvis de Chavannes, something clicked between male and female—a current, a chemical affinity, a radar impulse, a spark or a conflagration of fulfillment. Some mornings later, I lingered longer than my companions for an extra bottle of Bordeaux Paul and an extra helping of ripe Brie, to follow the duck-egg omelet with Brussels sprouts, I had already relished.

Nothing that develops later should make the reader forget that, as a cook, Philomène was an artist comparable with Madame Gillotte herself, and better than Monsieur, who never did anything more than moderately well. In dealing with sprouts, for instance, the wench would wash and trim them beyond any possibility that a single speck of grit would remain, then boil them not more than twelve minutes; and, after draining them faithfully and drying out most of the moisture in the pan, she

would brown them in butter to a perfection of
green and brown worthy of Chardin. A keen cru-
ciferous aroma blended with superior scorched fat
would pervade the proximity. In France many of
the present-day Jezebels and Queens of Shadow
have a deft hand with the skillet and the better
known and exotic seasonings.

Alone in that snug back room, at three in the
morning, I sensed that Philomène, who had never
paid special attention to me and, in fact, had
seemed to know by virtue of some extrasensory
perception that I missed little of what she did and
had detected the larceny in her heart, wanted words
with me, on a subject too confidential to deal with
directly. She hummed and fluttered. Naturally, I
made it easy for her. I remarked that it was selfish
to drink alone, and offered her her choice of liquid
refreshment. She fidgeted and squirmed, insisting that
the first swallow of anything strong undermined
her judgment, dispersed the guards who stood
watch over her virtue, then made her ill. Most
Frenchwomen are like that about liquor. The most
abandoned as well as the most modest wife and
mother protest when invited to drink. They feel
complimented, for instance, if one orders champagne for them, since champagne is expensive and
an outlay of cash or credit gives any gesture a solid
aspect that cannot be ignored. Philomène ended up
on the stuffed bench beside me, calf to pants leg,

with a sticky Italian liqueur called "Fiori d'Alpino" and helped herself coyly to a morsel of my bread and cheese.

"It is risky to drink without eating," she said.

I stood pat and let her flounder for a while. Somehow, as I had anticipated, the conversation tacked and hawed until we were talking of Monsieur Bernardi. He was a kind of an Englishman mixed with Italian, was he not? I put her at her ease by telling her gravely that most Australians were descendants of murderers, traitors and thieves who had been deported from England. I had her believing for a moment that Australia was a kind of English Devil's Island, and that Bernardi was one of the few who had managed to get out of there alive.

Philomène smiled, and some barriers were down.

"*C'est vrai.* He's a rascal," she agreed.

"He's mad about you," I volunteered. "You'd better watch out."

She looked at me solemnly.

"I'm going to demand a night off," she said. "Which one would you advise?"

"He's off on Thursdays," I told her.

The first Thursday off, Bernardi took Philomène to a movie called *Carnet de Bal* and the part she liked best was the episode in which the former dance partner of the heroine was drunk, abusive and had an epileptic fit.

Meanwhile, the innuendoes Philomène had planted

among neighbors and customers, which had badg-
ered Madame Gillotte into hiring a room for Bobo
in the attic of the adjacent building, caused Madame
Gillotte, when she had time to be a doting anxious
mother, misgivings and perplexities. The most sympathetic and intelligent confidante available was a
regular customer, one Marthe Doucet, a tall, sad-
eyed, pale-faced woman who wore black becom-
ingly. Marthe had noble features and impressive
stature. Her mouth seemed to indicate an unusual
capacity for suffering and surviving.

Marthe was the *sous-maîtresse* (sub-manager) of
the house of ill fame just around the corner in the
rue Rochechouart. Since part of Marthe's many
duties, all of which were technically respectable,
including shopping for girls and the staff of Mme
Marcelle's excellent lupanar, she had arranged with
Madame Gillotte to get many articles of food at
wholesale prices for her. Adding tips and various
prerogatives to her salary, Marthe made about $8
a week, plus a free room and her meals, which in
that grade of joy houses were appetizing and nour-
ishing. The girls who served the clients were mostly
somewhat restless by nature, and, having so many
houses to choose from, changed places frequently.
On the average, they made about $15 a week, more
than the salary of a veteran cashier in an established
bank.

Salaried workers in France do not dream of

becoming millionaires or Presidents of the Republic by virtue of thrift and patience. The lowest brackets, before the war, had to keep body and soul together on about $250 a year. City girls, therefore, who are poor and good-looking, accept middle-class men, married or otherwise, as "protectors," to help stabilize the economic situation and balance their budgets. Some prefer being aided or kept; others found organized prostitution a bearable steppingstone in the days before the post-war "reforms" drove them underground, but not too far. The more resourceful, and the unluckiest, have to proceed as free lances in a field where competition is fierce and the hazards are many.

Marthe Doucet had been in a position to observe the behavior of men and women in their unguarded hours, and under revealing circumstances. She was not unduly cynical and had retained, while gaining much wisdom, a lively sense of humor. To see Marthe and Madame Gillotte, side by side, in conversation, was to grasp that they were fine examples of French womanhood, in different lines of endeavor. Both were frank, honest, fair, hard working, thrifty and friendly. Madame Gillotte knew the restaurant business. Marthe Doucet was an expert on certain kinds of human relationships between male and female and the types in between. When the question had arisen, at the time Madame Gillotte had consulted the priest, as to whether Bobo, aged

sixteen, should leave the parental bed and lodge
elsewhere, nearby, Marthe had agreed positively
that Bobo must have a bedroom of his own. Marthe,
when she learned that Philomène, who loathed
Madame Gillotte, occupied a bedroom in the same
attic which Bobo seemed about to inhabit by night,
was tempted to express to Madame Gillotte an
instinctive premonition that the arrangement was
risky.

Because Madame Gillotte had been so perturbed,
Marthe refrained from warning her. And when
Marthe thought more about the possibilities, she
concluded that Bobo, someday soon, would blunder
onto some facts of life and that if Philomène happened to be the party of the second part, what
difference did it make? Actually, Marthe believed,
on reflection, that Philomène was so enamored with
Monsieur Bernardi that she would not tempt Bobo,
even to annoy or inflame Madame Gillotte.

I was inclined to agree with Marthe, for on the
second Thursday that Bernardi and Philomène, both
free from work for the day, went out together,
they wound up in a plush-curtained third-floor
room in the Hotel Williams et du Brazil, off the
Square Montholon. Seventeen hours later, when
they emerged in time for Philomène to change
clothes and make her 6 P.M. deadline at Gillotte's,
she showed no signs of regret or disappointment.
Bernardi, never having been quite able to credit

what Philomène and others had said about her unusual condition, was triumphant almost to the point of being smug.

A couple in England who found each other congenial and wished to express their fondness in a corresponding way would not have been able to find hundreds, if not thousands, of hospitable hotels with trained personnel anxious to make them comfortable and put them at their ease. They even might have had to hire a Drive Yourself car, park somewhere out of reach of the sly and anti-social police, and attempt Philomène's delayed initiation in the cramped back seat, steeped in the aroma of ethyl gasoline. Or Bernardi would have had to borrow a friend's flat, only to find that the friend's estranged wife had run out of money and decided to surprise her husband in a weak moment and wheedle another stake for permanents, cosmetics and low-calorie provender. Happily, Bernardi and Philomène were in France, where lovers' needs are understood and fulfilled in terms of objective reality.

Rabelais, who was as French as anyone could be, has a long debate with himself, in writing of the adventures of Panurge, as to whether the old game is more enjoyable if snatched by stealth, perchance in a haystack or the medieval equivalent of a telephone booth, with the fair wench smelling of common soft soap; or in the Oriental fashion, on a divan, at leisure, with a slave to give chase to the flies that tend to gather round about, and with musicians to be heard but not seen. Your Frenchman, if he is vigorous, will pursue almost any maiden—stranger or familiar, forward or shy—and until he has had her and they are *en rapport*, will, if in the country, make shift as opportunity affords. In a city—like Paris, Lyons, Dijon, Nancy, Tours, Marseilles, etc., etc.—he becomes very adept at luring coy partners into well-equipped hotels where no questions are asked and no item essential to aiding and abetting seduction is withheld.

In the latest Kinsey report on the habits of American women, a recapitulation showed that half of the women interviewed had enjoyed dalliance with men outside the provisions of laws, conventions or sanction by clergy. One in four of the married women interviewed had not been technically "true" to their husbands or their vows, one hundred per cent, all the time. The Frenchwomen quoted in the press of several countries, concerning these statistics, agreed that if Kinsey had studied conditions in France, he would have raised his percentages. In fact, the French commentators believed that about fifty per cent of their married women had adventured beyond the limits prescribed by convention. Who would assume that too many of them were the worse for having obeyed their impulses? Marriage, in France, is still an institution. Girls are not expected to select young men for whom they may feel an unusual sexual attraction. The parents and families of the predominant middle class still arrange marriages they think are suitable and advantageous. In any country where mates of the younger generation are paired by older folks, love and marriage are distinct, one from the other.

In the United States, boys and girls, men and women, couple in the haphazard fashion not too extravagantly caricatured by the boy-and-girl Hollywood films. English customs are somewhat in between those of France and North America. It seems to me that everywhere men are naturally promiscuous, and that women in love think of extramarital relations with real distaste or even horror. Of all peoples with whom I have come in contact, the French have the soundest and most wholesome ideas and understanding of sex, love, fidelity or philandering.

Tens of thousands of nice Frenchwomen somehow get detached from their families and others who naturally would feel responsible for their wellbeing. Of those, Marthe Doucet was a brave example. As a young girl she lived mostly in a convent, from the age of three to fourteen, under the guidance of her family in Troyes. That the monotonous discipline under the nuns or ex-nuns did not drain her of initiative and will to resist is a tribute to her character. It is noteworthy here, to keep the reader constantly reminded, that any attempt to regiment Frenchmen or women is doomed to failure at the start. That is the principal reason why those of us who feel close to and love the French (principally their institutions, and selected individuals) have no fear that France will embrace communism, or tolerate it.

The French "Communists" of today belong to a couple of militant trade unions. Their apparent strength at the polls and their rather large, but impotent, representation in the *Assemblée Nationale*, is not a sign of Moscow's growing influence or encroachments. It reflects a legitimate protest on the part of industrial labor and low-paid government employees who are still denied a decent living in return for hard work.

The middle-class French who are *déclassé* do not form organizations or join them. Each individual carries on a never-ending struggle to "defend" himself or herself, that is, to eat, sleep, wear clothes and live.

The women of the Corre family, in connection with the Hotel Bretagne, have never been faced with such stark problems and it is extremely unlikely that they ever will, unless another world war ruins all of us. The majority of middle-class families, like the Corres, are relatively "safe." Each member works hard and steadily in the common interest of the family or clan and is quite adequately rewarded, more by stability than wealth. Their social position will not change.

The group, which may be as large or larger, like the Gillottes, drive themselves unmercifully, for objectives which are new, therefore improvised. They are determined, and have reasonable expectation of starting their sons and daughters on a level above their own, as far as education and finances go.

Madame Marcelle, from the profits of her disorderly house (so very well conducted), was accumulating a large dowry for herself to the end that, eventually, she could marry a minor official in the government railway service, and live like a lady at a safe distance from Paris, where her popularity, the scope of her acquaintances and the nature of her activities might prove embarrassing. Marcelle and her railway man probably had children who enjoyed the principal advantages to enable them to fit into the French upper middle class.

Most certainly Marthe Doucet did not plan to have children, although in many ways she was the most sympathetic, worthy and attractive of the women I have used as examples. Marthe was one of those, in any society which functions largely as a collection of families, who has been cut off by circumstances from family co-operation and aid. In nearly all French families there is a stray, a ne'er-do-well, a superior, a sinner who gets caught, in short, a member who does not function in a family way. Some of the so-called demi-mondaines are in that category. In dim cheap rooms, obscure and solitary, are bachelors or fugitives from domesticity.

Some of the Frenchmen and women who operate on a solitary basis are eccentric; others seem to have been isolated from their natural environments by an unusual gift of common sense. Marthe did not venture out on her own from choice. Her mother had a jealous dislike of her because, as long as Monsieur Doucet lived, Marthe was his favorite. Unluckily for Marthe, her father was caught by her mother in an unquestionably compromising position with a shapely female employee, so the mother made her husband's life difficult to the end, and carried over and exercised her resentment on young Marthe, who had known about her father's liaison and from loyalty to him had not disclosed it. Eventually the mother married Marthe to a man so mean that he obliged her to walk, carrying her valise, from the Gare du Nord in Paris to the honeymoon hotel he had selected, because he could get reduced rates a mile from the station. Marthe, until that day of her wedding and departure from Troyes, had never even crossed the street from the family *Café du Théâtre*, in the public park at Troyes, to their second-floor apartment only fifty yards away. Her mother had tended the cash box in the *Café du Théâtre*, and kept an old aunt handy to take Marthe home during the short vacations she had from the convent.

Marthe's first husband kept her without funds, never once took her to a play or out for refreshments, bought her no clothes, and systematically bullied her out of the dowry her father had worked years in order to save. Since De Gaulle, Frenchwomen cannot be kicked around and victimized quite as easily as in the old days under the Code Napoléon. Compared with Italian women, for example, they are relatively as much freer and farther advanced in modernity as an osprey over the ocean has more liberty and scope than a capon in a pen. But the Frenchwomen, immeasurably stronger and more resourceful than the men, have suffered all handicaps of tradition and law, with Church and reactionary State like millstones round their necks, and have held their superior position, their real dominance, by stamina and stealth. The First World War did not do much to equalize privilege between the sexes in France. World War II has done more, particularly in areas where women worked shoulder to shoulder with men in the resistance and the underground. The labor unions, also, have raised factory women to a more dignified status, even though in doing so they have made French Communists out of many of them.

If ever there was a kind, well-meaning woman, Marthe Doucet was she, but with her back to the wall, trapped in a marriage which was drearier than convent life, cut off from her loving father by his death, unwelcome with her mother, who was afraid she would cost her a few sous, this tall quite regal-looking Frenchwoman, in her middle twenties, found no way out except to destroy her husband, day by day. Marthe was warned by the doctor to whom her husband had to go that rich foods would be fatal to him if he continued to indulge in them.

After meditation through long afternoons and dull evenings, with only a meager allowance for marketing and keeping the apartment near St. Laurent, on the rue du Désir off the Boulevard de Strasbourg, Marthe borrowed from her dear sister, Margaret, who was the only relative she had who was close to her and loved her wholeheartedly, enough money to buy a second-hand Escoffier. Marthe learned to cook like a master, with all the seasonings, wines, aromatics, pungents, condiments and spices. She succeeded so well that her husband, a gourmet, often came close to praising her, and was nearly affectionate sometimes. She tempted him with a patience and disarming solicitude almost divine, had its intention not been Satanic.

In two years and three months he died, and left Marthe without money or resources. Her convent education was less than useless in the world of toil; so she got work as cook in a small restaurant in the rue des Rosiers, a poor district in the old ghetto.

There Marthe made the acquaintance of Madame Croque, who ran the employment bureau for prostitutes and bawdy-house personnel. Madame Croque advised Marthe to quit cooking in cheap restaurants while she still had her looks and health, and to try some high-class bordel as sub-mistress, in which job she could be completely respectable.

That was how Marthe Doucet found her profession, but she met, alas, in the restaurant where she slaved over the hot ranges, a hold-up man who beat her so severely that she believed him when he said he would kill her if she did not marry him. It took a week for Marthe to get away from that one, to whom she remains married, in the sight of France, if not of God, until this day, when she is approaching eighty, and is working hard as a children's nurse for practically nothing, in the house of a nephew who is nice to her, and a nephew's wife who delights in finding fault.

It must not be assumed, from this bleak outline of Marthe's life that she has not lived, loved and transcended much suffering. She is calm, impressive, well-preserved, quite free of superstition, dread of death, or the hereafter.

When she went to work in her first lupanar, in the rue Mazet, 6th *arrondissement*, she concealed the nature of her employment from her sister Margaret, who was married and had a little niece Marthe idolized. But one day Margaret found it necessary to consult Marthe during working hours, and on discovering that the address of what Marthe had told her marked a linen shop was equipped with colored fan-light windows and bore the legend "*Entrez sans frapper,*" the fond elder sister wept and prayed. But she entered, and found Marthe's functions were not those described by the Victorians as "worse than death." Marthe's duties required presence and tact, but less effort than any other work available to her.

On her day off each week, Marthe visited Margaret, always bringing a present for little Margo, the niece who loved her so spontaneously. Margaret's husband, selected by the same mother who had picked Marthe's now defunct tyrant, was a paperhanger, a trade which had not then, because of Hitler, fallen into disrepute. For paperhangers there were slack seasons; so Margaret rented a spare room to an Italian who played trombone in the band at the *Cirque d'Hiver*. This Italian trombonist was tall, dark and handsome, and an accomplished *raconteur*. While the paperhanger husband was out, either at work or soliciting it, Margaret found that listening to Lorenzo's tales of a circus musician's life helped pass the time and lighten the tasks she could do while being thus entertained. Marthe, when she first met this Italian, felt a bewildering affinity, and so instead of spending her off-days and evenings elsewhere, began to enjoy the company of the Italian roomer in Margaret's house or, later, at the circus for which he obtained for her a free pass.

That was Marthe's real womanly awakening. She began to sing about her work, in her rich contralto voice which, at times, was reminiscent of Yvonne George. She spent some of her precious "economies" (that is how the French describe "savings") on new clothes, down to the skin. Her skin felt alive, her eyes were alight. The girls of the bordel, some of whom were inclined to melancholy, an occupational hazard such girls must risk, basked in her cheerful presence. The proprietress and owner, Madame Fifi, trusted Marthe more and more, and often left Paris for the country, where she would spend a week or ten days, certain that Marthe would keep true accounts and run the establishment in an exemplary way.

The clients of the bordel began to let their attention stray from the line-up of girls offered for their choice, and few of the live ones failed to make an attempt to date up Marthe outside. None of them succeeded, and all knew why. She was a satisfied woman.

Marthe was still in certain ways as naïve as when she had attended the convent. That is, she was not on her guard and did not suspect that the man she loved would trick her in any way. When the trombonist asked her not to mention to her sister Mar-

garet that he had given her (Marthe) a permanent
free pass to the circus, Marthe accepted his explanation that a performer in the band was entitled only
to one such prerogative, intended for his wife. He
did not want to hurt Margaret's feelings, for after
all he had known Margaret first.

Somehow Marthe's circus pass slipped out of
her purse and Margaret saw it. Margaret inquired,
cautiously, and when Marthe poured out to her
older sister the rich tale of her affair with the Italian,
Margaret fainted dead away. The Italian, of course,
had got around Margaret, too, and convinced her
she was the only woman in the world who fascinated him. He had sworn that he would destroy
himself if Margaret did not yield, and Margaret
had found raptures—comparable with those of
Marthe—it appeared later, when Margaret was
strong enough to compare notes. Actually Margaret
was ill a long time. The Italian moved over to the
Cirque Médrano and found another rooming house,
with an attractive married woman in charge. Marthe,
unable to face her admiring prostitutes in Madame
Fifi's house any longer, since they had become
dependent on her for sustaining a gay *morale*, had
a tearful session with Madame Fifi, who was so
dismayed at losing Marthe that she was never polite
to an Italian again. Thus fate had brought Marthe,
through the machinations of Madame Croque's em-

ployment bureau, over to Madame Marcelle, in the quarter of the *Métro* Cadet, and into the circle of the Gillottes.

There is no knowing who would have been chosen as a confidante by Madame Gillotte had not Marthe found bliss and pain on the fringe of the old ghetto in the Temple Quarter. As I have stated already, Marthe was firm and positive in advising that Bobo should have a bed away from his mother's. She was on the point of warning Mme Gillotte that Philomène's presence on the other side of a very thin wall, nightly, might prove a hazard. Then we all saw that Philomène was madly in love with Bernardi, having joined through him the great majority of women who, on some terms or others, had parted with perhaps the only attribute or asset they could neither replace nor recall, which nevertheless did not, when removed, inflict a fatal injury. Had Bernardi been planning a stationary career, he might have had qualms or worries about Philomène's intensity. But he expected, once he had purchased the requisite press notices, and starred at the *Comique*, to roam the British Empire, and, if possible, the United States. He was traveling light and certainly could match any of Longfellow's Arabs, if it came to a quick getaway.

As day off followed day on, Bernardi was more content and less cagey, for Philomène not only refrained from throwing out hints of a possible marriage but declared she did not believe in the institution. She maintained that couples should stay together only while united by a compelling urge. Marriage, Philomène declared, was sordid, synthetic, material and tiresome. She had escaped it, had achieved maturity, and was happier than any wife in the land.

Meanwhile Bobo, who always had to be doing something obstructive, got himself expelled from the Sorbonne. Nearly everyone at the Sorbonne cheated in the course of written examinations, but Bobo was so clumsy about it that no instructor could overlook his cribbing and preserve an appearance of fairness and discipline. After that, Bobo, who could not sleep all the hours, and cared nothing for reading, drinking, sports or agreeable vices, in sheer boredom was forced to volunteer to help his mother and father in the *bistrot*. The pride and joy with which Madame Gillotte announced this to each of us, separately and privately, was touching indeed. By the time she had finished, it appeared to us, as no doubt it did to her, that Bobo, sacrificing a career to lighten the burden of toil on his parents in their middle age, had decided, without prompting, that he would be a restaurant keeper, and that what had been good enough for his parents would be right for him.

The first evening that Bobo helped serve dinner, I was sitting next to Bernardi among our colleagues of the *Chicago Tribune*. I ordered *potage St. Germain*, after my radishes with butter, and Bobo tilted most of it on a new jacket and trousers which had set back Bernardi $15 in francs, about two months' pay. He had an important audition coming up for which the neat new suit was *de rigueur*. Also, his weekly excursions into Cythera with Philomène had strained his finances sorely. He had borrowed from any of us who had an extra hundred francs, was behind with his room rent, and owed a sizable pile to the Gillottes, as who of us did not.

Bobo, so fat and sorry, his soft face quivering with regret, was not the type one could curse and berate. Bernardi turned scarlet, then white, and Philomène was instantly all over him with damp cloths and hot water and cleaning fluid, which in France just then was more inflammable than ether. Our sports editor, Egan, was immersed in reflections of his own (which were sure to involve women and/or horses) so he was unaware of the situation which had developed around him and casually thumbed a cigarette lighter.

His cigarette was about the only object in that vicinity that was not set aflame. In putting out the intimate flash fire, we overturned the table with dishes, wine, food, implements and everything. Gillotte's back room was a shambles.

There were occasions after that when Bobo's gift for disorganization had less spectacular results, but in that small saloon and eating house, where each foot of space had been given its use through years of trial and error, Bobo's bulk—he was then 5 feet 10 inches high and had a circumference of about 45 inches—became a new factor with which all hands must reckon.

Madame Gillotte was anxious to make amends for the damage to Bernardi's new suit, and did so handsomely. The catch was, as far as Bernardi was concerned, that he owed Madame Gillotte a bit more than the price of the suit. The debt was canceled but still he had no suit and no cash.

Late that night, Bernardi, in his ruined suit, now scorched as well as stained, was brooding at Gillotte's, with gin and *gazeuse,* the nearest thing to gin and tonic obtainable in the quarter Cadet. Philomène slid to the bench by his side, so charged with affection that Bernardi could have felt it through the thickness of three or four suits. She assured him that she had been able to make many "economies" since coming to Paris, and that she would be hurt to the quick if he would not accept a loan from her to buy a new suit, to help him to fame and fortune.

Bernardi had strict ideas about taking money from females when the prospect of repayment in cash was too slim to be considered. He stubbornly demurred. She wept and declared he did not love her, that Englishmen were cold and cruel, etc., etc.

I think Bernardi could have withstood the charge that he, himself, was cold, but the slur on the Empire stung him. He agreed to take the money. Philomène did not have it on her. It was to be delivered on their day off, Thursday, which was two days away.

Before Philomène yielded to Bernardi, at the age of forty, her appearance at Gillotte's, so shapely, so colorful and seriously coy, prompted the editors and employees of two newspapers, the *Chicago Tribune* and the *Petit Journal*, to offer her extravagant inducements for her favors. Some of these men of dishonorable intentions were English, some American, many were French, and there was at least one Rumanian, one Czech, three White Russians (one technically a woman) and a Turk. Besides those, Philomène had her choice of all the Italians in and around the neighborhood wine shop. They numbered about two dozen, and most of them, instead of offering to pay money, expected one way or another to collect for the rapture they would give her. There was an unacquisitive exception, however: one of the aides in the Italian Embassy. Like others of his countrymen he set immense store by virginity, and would rather deflower one sub-average little schoolgirl than have the whole chorus at the Follies free of charge. Signor Dragonetti was important among his compatriots, and threw his weight around. He had been so sure of

captivating Philomène that he had announced his
intentions in advance, and the jibes he had to endure from his fellow-Italians of the neighborhood
and in diplomatic circles when Philomène turned
him down flat would have sent a man of less stamina
to an institution.

At five o'clock that Wednesday morning, after
Bernardi had lost his suit of clothes, the telephone
in the residence of Signor Dragonetti rang, and
a timid voice said something that brought him
blithely out of bed. At Gillotte's, once Bernardi
had gone to his lone bedroom, feeling relief mingled
with shame at having agreed to accept Philomène's
savings, to be repaid when he became world-
famous, Philomène told Monsieur Gillotte that she
had a migraine headache, of the kind that would
last two days. He let her off, of course.

Someone, discreetly hooded with a scarf, entered
Dragonetti's residence by the garden gate at dawn.
Dragonetti's butler informed the Ambassador that
his aide was confined to his bed but would try to
report on Thursday. On Thursday, Philomène, a
little bewildered because the experience had proven
not loathsome but instructive and delightful, gave
Bernardi the promised money.

Dragonetti, once he had "possessed" Philomène,
who by devices known only to her gave him the
illusion that he was the first, was fairly discreet for
an Italian. He did not want his chief, the Ambassa-

dor, to find out that the indisposition which had kept him from work on a busy Wednesday had its origin in *amour*. For the Ambassador, in a similar instance involving another aide, had insisted on being introduced to the lady in question and had exercised a modern form of the *droit du seigneur*. But fate would have it that Dragonetti was a circus fan, and thus was well acquainted with Marthe's Signor Lorenzo, the trombonist in the band. Over cups, following a performance at the *Cirque Médrano*, Dragonetti told Lorenzo about the *Bistrot Gillotte*, of the appearance of a mature and ravishing virgin, of the contest resembling a tourney of old, and of how he, Dragonetti, had carried off on his lance the lady's colors. Had he stopped there, all might have gone better. Instead he became voluble about other rare customers of the Gillotte *bistrot*, mentioning by name Marthe Doucet, the charming but sad *sous-maîtresse* of the *Bordel de Madame Marcelle* in the rue Rochechouart.

On hearing the name of Marthe, who had fled from him broken-hearted, the trombonist, Lorenzo, upset a nearly full bottle of fine Piedmont wine, and trembled so violently that Dragonetti thought his friend had caught malaria.

The scene shifts to the disorderly house, so piquant and well-appointed, of Madame Marcelle. Madame Marthe had retired for her short period of evening rest, before the rush of after-hour business. The Italian trombonist, seemingly a madman, rushed through the street doorway, marked *"Entrez sans frapper,"* took the carpeted stairway three steps at a time, burst into the reception room where a startled broker was looking over a bevy of adult midget girls dressed as school children, with bows in their hair in pigtails, and shouted "I demand to see Marthe!"

Madame Marcelle and the bouncer, who later made quite a name as a French screen actor, had Lorenzo in a curtained anteroom before anyone could say "Knife." But one of the girls in the girls' waiting room heard the cry for Marthe, slipped up to the second floor and roused Marthe, who nearly fainted. Marthe tried to get her nightgown off and some other clothes on, but her shaking limbs and fingers would not coordinate.

Down in the anteroom Lorenzo was pleading with Marcelle and the bouncer, both of whom were sentimental to a fault. He convinced, in less than two minutes, the worldly landlady and the athletic and handsome young bouncer that he was insane with love for Marthe, who had forsaken him and concealed herself from him through a tragic misunderstanding.

Madame Marcelle, with a gesture, sent the trombonist upstairs, saying "Third door to the right, monsieur, if monsieur will be quiet."

Lorenzo took the second flight of stairs four at

a time, and, in his excitement miscounted the doors to the right, thus crashing into the room occupied by Mme Jarry, the house cook, who screamed and started running around the room.

The din caused Marthe in the next room actually to swoon, so that by the time Lorenzo had realized his mistake and crashed into the proper room, he was just in time to catch Marthe's senseless form. His ardor was such that when she regained consciousness, it was too late for any practicable remonstrance, even if she had had it in her stricken heart to attempt it. Before dawn he had convinced her that his attentions to Margaret, Marthe's sister, had been merely the result of his drinking a bit too much grappa. What could Marthe do but forgive him, and resume what she realized must be an impermanent affair, in which she would suffer at the end.

The trombonist could not resist telling Marthe about Signor Dragonetti's conquest of the red-headed "virgin" who worked in a neighboring *bistrot*. Marthe passed on the item to me, knowing I would be amused, as she was, to learn that Philomène's attachment to Bernardi was not as complete as it had appeared. I connected the incident with the money Philomène had forced on Bernardi for the suit he must have in connection with the critical audition.

In describing the daily lives of the members of the
Corre family who owned the Hotel Bretagne in a
quiet secluded quarter near St. Sulpice, within a
stone's throw of St. Germain des Prés, at present
the center and focus of the rather feverish night
life of Paris, I tried to suggest the mode and attri-
butes and shortcomings of upper-middle-class life
in France. Jean Corre, at the age of forty, was ad-
mirably equipped to carry on the business, the tradition, the social convictions and the complaints of
his father Valentin, who came to Paris from Brittany just after the disastrous Franco-Prussian War
of 1870. From the time he established his hotel he
grumbled until the day of his death about the
weight of taxes he carried following the peace dic-
tated by Bismarck. Now, Jean, able and eager to
manage a prosperous hotel business, gripes, and with
even more justification, against post-war taxes, political instability, maladjustment and the general
national economic collapse.

Far from the St. Sulpice quarter and the Hotel
Bretagne, in distance and in spirit, over on the right
bank at the foot of Montmartre near the *Métro*
Cadet, are the family I found to be typical of the
lower middle class. The Gillottes—father, mother
and son—and the social milieu they represent are as
far removed from St. Sulpice, which soars to the
upper reaches of their own class, as the Corres are

interdicted from dwelling in that astral world known as the Etoile.

With these distinctions in mind, it is possible to begin to understand the stratification of French society, even if it is impossible to peel apart the layer upon layer upon layer of each division.

The Gillottes worked the clock around to advance, if not themselves, their unco-operative son. Only in this sense did they try to promote themselves socially. Their aspirations were finally and irretrievably shattered when Bobo began, in his sluggish and inept manner, to cast a half-opened but lustful eye on Philomène. Bernardi, the Italian-Australian tenor, had said good-bye forever to her, pleading the ageless conflict between love and a career, such as it was. The forsaken Philomène seemed to accept his choice as inevitable if not exactly desirable. Her customers and well-wishers could not fail to notice that she was taking her abandonment with good grace and were curious to know the reasons for her serenity. Soon their curiosity was changed to astonishment. Philomène eloped with Bobo and married him!

The only way we could account for so desperate a measure was that Philomène hoped to acquire the savings accumulated by the elder Gillottes and could hurt and humiliate Madame Gillotte while doing so.

Monsieur and Madame Gillotte, thwarted from

lifting their son a notch higher in the social scale, sold their Paris *bistrot* and went back to the Midi, where they could endure their disappointment without having to make explanations to present and former customers. Unable to remain inactive after so many years of strenuous work, they ventured into the restaurant and café business again, somewhere near Moulins. Their struggle is lonely and grim.

One thing keeps Madame Gillotte alive: she is determined to survive Philomène. Failing, by accident or an act of God, in that resolution, she has made provision that all her savings be tied up so that Bobo will not get any portion of the money while Philomène is near enough to take it away from him.

Philomène and Bobo work in a man-and-wife job as concierges of a Paris apartment building, where Philomène enjoys her contacts with the police and the opportunity to provide them with whatever gossip she can pick up from her station at the entrance to the multiple dwelling house. She prods and scolds Bobo continuously but to no avail as far as inducing him to do any work is concerned. When he can escape Philomène's vigilance, Bobo visits his parents, but he is afraid to stay away too long. He still tries to wheedle money from his doting but now sadder and wiser mother.

There are millions of families and hundreds of

quarters in Paris. Each neighborhood, however un-distinguished by ordinary standards, will yield rich treasures upon examination and help make France and the French understandable and kindred to all mankind.

The unique virtue of Parisians, native or resident by choice, is that even a limited acquaintance with a few of them offers insights into the nature of a diverse, complex but always enlightened people. They are responsive to ideas, to art and to amenity. To understand these dwellers in the city of light and those who give character to the cities and prov-inces it is only necessary to want to share with them their belief in their own trinity of Liberty, Equality, Fraternity, in the order named.

ELLIOT PAUL, author of *Understanding the French* and twenty-six other books, was born in Malden, Massachusetts, on February 11, 1891. His boyhood was spent in the bosom of a conservative New England family, but an unappeasable wanderlust carried him all over the world. He joined his older brother as a timekeeper and surveyor on an irrigation project in Idaho and Wyoming and after several jobs in construction camps in the Northwest, he enlisted in the AEF. He decided to remain in France after the Armistice. Off and on he lived on the rue de la Huchette, that street so lovingly celebrated in *The Last Time I Saw Paris*, for eighteen years. With Eugene Jolas he founded *transition*, the startling and distinguished avant-garde magazine of the Parisian expatriates. In 1931 Elliot Paul went to live in Santa Eulalia, Ibiza, in the Balearic Islands. The story of an idyllic life wantonly destroyed was told in *The Life and Death of a Spanish Town*.

The outbreak of World War II brought

the novelist back to New York, where he scored an immediate success with his first detective story, *The Mysterious Mickey Finn*. There followed a half-dozen accounts of the prodigious exploits of his debonair detective, Homer Evans.

Now living in California, Elliot Paul devotes himself to the writing of his unorthodox autobiography in many volumes under the generic title of *Items on the Grand Account* and to books that pay tribute to his second homeland—France.